A Market in Airport Slots

A Market in Airport Slots

KEITH BOYFIELD (EDITOR),
DAVID STARKIE, TOM BASS,
BARRY HUMPHREYS

The Institute of Economic Affairs

First published in Great Britain in 2003 by
The Institute of Economic Affairs
2 Lord North Street
Westminster
London SW1P 3LB
in association with Profile Books Ltd

A CIP catalogue record for this book is available from the British Library.

ISBN 0 255 36505 5

Many IEA publications are translated into languages other than English or
are reprinted. Permission to translate or to reprint should be sought from the
General Director at the address above.

Typeset in Stone by MacGuru Ltd
info@macguru.org.uk

Printed and bound in Great Britain by Hobbs the Printers

CONTENTS

AUTHORS

Keith Boyfield

Keith Boyfield is a graduate of the London School of Economics. He is a consultant economist who specialises in competition and regulatory issues. He advises a range of multinational companies, trade associations and non-profit organisations, and has acted as a consultant to several companies in the civil aviation sector, including BAA. He has also written extensively on airline competition and airport policy issues, and given written and oral evidence to the House of Commons Select Committee on Transport. His study on *The Impact of No Frills Carriers on the European Scheduled Airline Market* was published as the second volume in the Sources of Competitiveness series by the Chartered Institute of Marketing in December 2001. His earlier study on the case for feeder-reliever airports in the South-East, *Plane Commonsense*, was published by the Adam Smith Institute.

David Starkie

David Starkie is managing director of Economics-Plus Limited, London, and director of transport programmes at the Regulatory Policy Institute, Oxford. Apart from a two-year contract with the Western Australian government, when he served as deputy to the

Director General of Transport, he followed an academic career until 1985, leading up to the position of professorial fellow in the Department of Economics at the University of Adelaide. He has been a director of several economic consultancies and has undertaken work for both private and public sector clients, especially in the aviation sector, including the Civil Aviation Authority (CAA), the International Air Transport Association (IATA), the European Commission, BAA, British Airways, Qantas and Air New Zealand. He has worked extensively on the privatisation and regulation of airports in the UK, Australia, New Zealand and South Africa and, since early 2001, has been economic adviser to the Commission for Aviation Regulation, the regulator for Irish airports.

During his career he has also served on a number of government committees and, between 1972 and 1997, advised select committees of the House of Commons on more than a dozen inquiries covering wide-ranging subjects, including airline computer reservations systems (CRS), US/UK aviation bilaterals, and UK and EU aviation policies.

David Starkie is a member of the Royal Economic Society and of the Institute of Directors and an Associate of the American Bar Association. He is the author of many papers and books, including *Privatising London's Airports* (with David Thompson) and a study of the valuation of aviation noise, *The Economic Value of Peace and Quiet* (with David Johnson). He is also on the editorial board of the *Journal of Air Transport Management* and is an editor of the *Journal of Transport Economics and Policy*.

Tom Bass

After graduation from Oxford University, Tom Bass joined the

Economist Intelligence Unit, where he worked on industrial and transport projects in Europe, North America, Africa and the Far East. He became an economic adviser to the CAA in 1972, specialising in airline economics. He subsequently became Head of Economics, Statistics and Airports Policy, and in that capacity was responsible for the five-yearly reviews of the BAA London and Manchester airports and for the regulation of airports' conduct.

Since leaving the CAA in 1997, Tom Bass has worked as a senior consultant with the Portland Group (now part of Macquarie Bank) and for other clients on the economic regulation of airports. These include a range of international airports such as Amsterdam, Berlin, Jakarta, Wellington and, most recently, Kingston and Montego Bay in Jamaica.

Barry Humphreys

Barry Humphreys received a BA in Economics/Economic History from the University of Leicester and a PhD in Air Transport Economics from the University of Leeds. He spent many years with the CAA, eventually becoming Head of Air Services Policy and a member of the CAA's Senior Management Group. In 1995, he joined Virgin Atlantic Airways as Director of External Affairs and Route Development. He has written numerous papers and studies on the subject of air transport regulation and continues to lecture widely on the subject.

FOREWORD

During the 1980s and 1990s a number of countries privatised their airports, although a substantial number remain in public ownership. The results of privatisation are obvious to the airports' customers: airports have become clean, efficient and vibrant retail centres. Many airlines have also been privatised, again with substantial benefits to customers.

Airlines' customers probably do not realise that 'behind the scenes' the market is largely absent. Insofar as take-off and landing slots are concerned, property rights are not properly established, pricing is ad hoc and regulation intervenes to undertake tasks which could more properly be carried out by a market with properly delineated property rights and an economically rational pricing structure. The results of the status quo are predictable. There are serious economic inefficiencies from not pricing airport take-off and landing slots at economic cost. Congestion is evident and, arguably, environmental damage arises from not assigning and enforcing tradable property rights because users do not face the full economic cost of airport slots. Potential new entrants may be excluded from the market where informal property rights favour existing providers of airline services.

Reform of this system, however desirable, is not straightforward. The papers in this volume describe the problems of the status quo very effectively. They are also clear about the direction reform should take. Nevertheless, they are careful to point out the practical obstacles to reform and suggest ways round these obstacles. There will be difficulties in dealing with airlines that have invested on the assumption that they have implicit property rights in airport slots. There will also be potential competition issues if natural monopolies develop at particular airports as a result of the development of a market in airport slots.

But the message is clear. The needs of all those who have an interest in the efficient use of scarce airport facilities will be best served by the development of property rights in airport slots. Furthermore, those property rights should be tradable to ensure that slots are used by airlines, and ultimately customers, who value them most, and not just by existing players. The development of such a market could be of significant importance to air travellers, but also to those who are affected by airport congestion and the pressure to expand airport capacity.

Readings 56 begins with an editorial by Keith Boyfield. The editorial discusses the ideas of the other authors, David Starkie, Tom Bass and Barry Humphreys, and discusses the regulatory context at the national, European Union and international levels. Keith Boyfield also develops ideas of his own for reform. The editorial is followed by the papers of the other authors, each of which has a different perspective and comes to similar conclusions in principle but conclusions that differ in their practical detail. The authors' proposals to develop a market in airport slots are an important contribution to the debate that is taking place on this issue in many countries.

As in all IEA publications, the views expressed in Readings 56 are those of the authors, not those of the Institute (which has no corporate view), its managing trustees, Academic Advisory Council members or senior staff.

PHILIP BOOTH

Editorial and Programme Director,
Institute of Economic Affairs
Professor of Insurance and Risk Management,
Sir John Cass Business School, City University

SUMMARY

- Capacity at major international airports is under intense pressure. Currently Heathrow airport is handling 20 per cent more passengers than it was designed for, and Gatwick is operating at full capacity.

- A key aspect of the capacity and congestion problems is the apparent shortage of take-off and landing slots.

- In the European Union, take-off and landing slots at airports are generally allocated on a 'grandfathered' basis. Slots are granted to airlines that have used them historically.

- There is considerable pressure from well-established airlines to maintain this system.

- The existing system impedes competition and impedes the trading of slots to allow them to be used by airlines that would obtain the greatest value from them.

- It is highly likely that the absence of a market in airport slots leads to increased congestion at the most popular London airports and may provide false signals to them to expand.

- US experience suggests that a secondary market in airport slots could bring significant advantages.

- For such a market to operate, property rights over slots and a framework in which the market could work need to be properly established.

- There are special features of the airline industry that

dictate the precise approach to liberalisation. In particular, competition issues must be appropriately dealt with, and it may need to be recognised that airlines have made investments based on the assumption that they have established property rights to airport slots. None of these issues overrides the need to establish a secondary market in airport slots.

- The trading of slots in such a secondary market would bring significant economic welfare benefits to consumers and, possibly, to those who are affected by airport congestion and expansion.

TABLES

A Market in Airport Slots

1 WHO OWNS AIRPORT SLOTS? A MARKET SOLUTION TO A DEEPENING DILEMMA

Keith Boyfield

Introduction

This collection of essays examines a highly controversial issue in civil aviation: who can claim the right to own slots at congested airports? This is a key question in an industry which is experiencing strong growth as a result of liberalisation within the European Union (EU). Demand for air travel in the UK is growing at a staggering rate, spurred on by the success of no-frills airlines.[1] In 1991, the total number of terminal passengers passing through the six airports in the Greater London area totalled 62.7 million. A decade later, the corresponding figure had increased to 113.4 million, even though air travel was severely hit by the 11 September 2001 atrocities (see Table 1).

Consequently, those who can lay claim to exercising a property right at congested airports enjoy a substantial competitive advantage over their rivals. However, the whole issue of property rights as they relate to airport slots remains confused. There is an essential need to clarify and define the rules that are employed to allocate these scarce resources at congested airports.

This collection sets out the views of three leading figures – Tom

---

1   See Keith Boyfield, *The Impact of No Frills Carriers on the European Scheduled Airline Market*, Chartered Institute of Marketing, Sources of Competitiveness series, Volume II, December 2001.

Bass, Barry Humphreys and David Starkie – all of whom have considerable experience of the economics of the civil aviation sector. The fact that their views differ, markedly on occasions, reflects the controversy surrounding this crucial issue in civil aviation.

The current confusion over slots

For many decades civil aviation was tightly controlled by governments. As a result, market forces were highly constrained since national governments – acting on their own and through bilateral air service agreements – controlled the number of carriers on a specific route, the frequency of service, the level of fares and effective profitability. Indeed, airlines often pooled revenues on an international service. In the 1980s and 1990s this tight regulatory control was gradually relaxed and civil aviation is now essentially deregulated in the US and the EU. Carriers can fly on any route in any country within the EU, so long as they are registered within a member state and meet the appropriate safety standards. Nonetheless, as Barry Humphreys points out in his paper, it remains the case that air transport is treated by governments as being 'special' and in need of protection. For example, a US airline cannot acquire a majority equity stake in a UK carrier, nor for that matter can a UK airline take over a US carrier. Governments' reluctance to allow mergers within the civil aviation industry has led to the emergence of global alliances where only a minority stake may be acquired in an airline.

Greater economic prosperity and regulatory liberalisation has led to an upsurge in demand for air travel. This has given rise to significant congestion problems at a number of major European hubs, most notably Heathrow, Paris CDG, Frankfurt and

Schiphol. Other large airports such as Gatwick are also effectively full for much of the day. Further details of the precise extent of congestion at European airports is provided in Table 4 in Barry Humphreys' paper.[2] What emerges from the picture sketched by Humphreys is a pressing problem with regard to lack of runway capacity. The dilemma is at its most extreme at London's two principal airports: Heathrow and Gatwick.

Capacity at Heathrow is under immense pressure. The two runways and four terminals are currently handling over 60 million passengers a year (see Table 1), yet the terminal capacity was originally designed to cope with a maximum of 50 million passengers a year.[3] In November 2001, the Secretary of State for Transport, Local Government and the Regions approved the development of a fifth passenger terminal, subject to a number of provisos, notably an annual limit of 480,000 on the number of flights at Heathrow once the new terminal is opened.

Meanwhile, Gatwick is limited by the fact that it has only one main runway. In only ten years passenger numbers have increased from just under 19 million in 1991 to over 31 million in 2001. For most of the day, the airport is operating at full capacity: it is now very difficult to obtain a new slot at Gatwick.

In the UK, the economics of congested airports differs from that of other markets for several reasons. Capacity is effectively controlled by the government through the planning process. The difficulties involved in winning planning approval are well known. It took more than eight years for BAA to win approval for its plans

---

2   IATA estimates that, within five years, no fewer than 25 European airports will be confronted with serious congestion problems.

3   See Keith Boyfield, *Plane Commonsense: The case for feeder-reliever airports in the South East*, Adam Smith Institute, 1994, p. 8.

to develop a fifth terminal at Heathrow. The planning inquiry was the longest ever held in Britain.

Since London's major airports were privatised as a monopoly, and a tight constraint has been placed on new capacity, political considerations have prevented the price mechanism from being allowed to function with regard to the allocation of scarce slots. Table 1 shows that BAA, the operator of Heathrow, Gatwick and Stansted, enjoys a 92.8 per cent share of the Greater London airport market. For many years, successive governments have treated the four London airports[4] as part of a system, rather than as free-standing airports competing with each other.

The only significant new entrant into the market in recent years has been LondonCity Airport. After a difficult start in which the airport owner, the Mowlem construction company, sustained losses of £70 million,[5] the facility was acquired in 1995 by Dermot Desmond, a former chairman of Air Rianta, the Irish airports authority. Mr Desmond paid £23.5 million for the airport, the surrounding land and freehold. It has proved a spectacularly successful investment. Passenger numbers have more than doubled since 1996, with the airport handling a total of 1,619,000 passengers in the calendar year 2001. Nine airlines use the airport, offering services to 22 European cities. However, London City Airport is small – it accounts for only 1.43 per cent of passenger traffic in the South-East region (see Table 1) – and it deliberately sets out to serve a specialised market, the business traveller wanting easy access to the City of London.

With Heathrow and Gatwick operating at or beyond capac-

---

4   The fourth being Luton, until recently wholly owned by the local authority.
5   See the *Financial Times*, 31 October 1995.

Table 1 **Passenger throughput at major airports in the South-East of England, 1 January–31 December 2001**

Airport	Terminal passengers	%
Heathrow (BAA)	60,454,000	53.33
Gatwick (BAA)	31,097,000	27.43
Stansted (BAA)	13,654,000	12.04
London City	1,619,000	1.43
London–Luton	6,540,000	5.77
TOTAL	113,367,000	100.00

Source: CAA.

ity, BAA has been keen to encourage airlines to fly into and out of Stansted, its third main airport in the South-East. The company argues that, without its monopoly, Stansted would never have been built. Certainly, income generated by Heathrow as well as Gatwick has cross-subsidised the development of Stansted. For many years, Stansted was empty: it was in the wrong location, a significant distance from the homes of most airport users, and there was little interlining traffic. It was this under-utilisation which made the airport so attractive to the growing number of no-frills carriers, such as Ryanair and go. Today, Stansted is the main centre for no-frills carriers, frequently offering exceptionally competitive fares to destinations throughout the UK and Europe. However, in terms of intercontinental flights, Heathrow and Gatwick effectively have a regional duopoly.

The regulatory price regime governing London's three main airports has encouraged this traffic pattern. Individual airports have not been allowed by the regulatory authorities to raise charges sufficiently to ration demand. Not only is it estimated that airport charges at Heathrow, Gatwick and Stansted are at least 25 per cent below those at Europe's other main hubs,[6]

6   'Airport charges', *Financial Times* editorial, 8 March 2002.

but the differences in departure charges at Heathrow, Gatwick and Stansted are also relatively limited. In terms of costs per passenger, it costs a carrier on average only £1 more to use Heathrow than either Gatwick or Stansted.[7] Yet carriers can typically earn an additional 15 to 20 per cent in terms of passenger yields at Heathrow, simply because of the interlining capacity at this major international hub. In contrast, Gatwick and Stansted are much smaller and a greater proportion of their traffic is accounted for by charter operations.

The 'single till' principle underpinning the current regulatory pricing regime compounds this trend since it bundles revenues from commercial activities such as landside retailing, car parking, etc., with revenues from landing charges, aircraft parking charges and per passenger charges, to arrive at an overall permissible rate of return.[8] Furthermore, airline charges at regulated UK airports have fallen in real terms.[9] Consequently, airlines clamour to use Heathrow because this has a significant impact on their profitability. The RUCATSE (runway capacity in the South-East) Report,

---

7   Interview with Ian McDougall, BAA Airport Pricing Manager, 26 January 2000.
8   In November 2002, having consulted with interested parties, the Competition Commission recommended a continuation of the current single till approach to airport regulation in the UK. Although the CAA had originally proposed that the single till approach should be dropped, it accepted the Competition Commission's recommendation to retain the single till regime for the five-year regulatory period beginning 1 April 2003. In a news release dated 29 November 2002, the CAA referred to the 'absence of strong support from market participants for a move away from a single till' approach. In a footnote to the news release, it was nevertheless pointed out that the Authority was 'also proposing that the CAA would have to be satisfied that such projects generate net benefits in terms of the CAA's statutory objectives'.
9   'The future of airport economic regulation', a presentation given by Doug Andrews, Group Director of Economic Regulation at the Civil Aviation Authority, Airport Operators Association conference, 12 October 1999.

published in 1993, suggested that the fares premium charged by airlines operating into and out of Heathrow might be equivalent to £20 per passenger.

As soon as airlines were given the chance to move operations to Heathrow, following the removal of the Air Traffic Rules in 1991, they did so. As Tom Bass observes, Virgin concentrated its high-yield services at Heathrow and operated its less profitable services from Gatwick. Similarly, BA transferred its lower-yield routes, including those serving South America, to Gatwick and used its spare slots for more profitable routes. It is claimed that charges might have to be raised by between seven to twenty times for there to be any significant change in carriers' demand preferences, as far as Heathrow is concerned. Certainly, Bass notes that 'the market-clearing price at Heathrow would have to be extremely high, in-volving large multiples of the present regulated charges'. However, no one really knows the elasticity of demand function for specific airports because it has never been tested.

It is no wonder that there is a high premium on scarce slots in the London airport system. Runway capacity is tightly con-strained; the monopoly provider of runway space is under no great incentive to construct new runway capacity since the current regu-latory pricing regime caps its potential profits; and, furthermore, the regulatory regime has the perverse effect of encouraging de-mand at Heathrow and Gatwick since slots are priced well below the market-clearing level. One of the more insidious effects of a sub-optimal pricing policy at congested hubs is to reduce the at-tractiveness to airlines of alternative airports, thus compounding the congestion problem.[10] In the meantime, incumbent airlines

---

10   To the author this remains perplexing: Stansted is a far more pleasant airport to use than either Heathrow or Gatwick.

that have established 'grandfathering' rights at the most crowded airports represent a vociferous interest group. They lobby vigorously in defence of their commercial interests. And the financial sums at stake are immense: incumbent airlines are benefiting from substantial monopoly rents since it would appear that passengers are prepared to pay high premiums to use Heathrow and, to a lesser extent, Gatwick.

The aborted BA/American Airlines alliance

The flaws that permeate the present system of allocating slots at congested airports were exposed by the long-drawn-out debacle over the proposed BA/American Airlines alliance. Both airlines had built up a major presence at the most popular London hub, Heathrow. Indeed, Virgin Atlantic argued that the proposed alliance would amount to over 60 per cent of the US/UK passenger market,[11] and there were widespread calls for the airlines to surrender slots. The EU Commissioner responsible for competition policy, Karel van Miert, was particularly anxious to ensure that the two alliance partners should surrender slots to rival airlines. Negotiations over the precise number of slots that might be surrendered raised the controversial question of whether BA and American Airlines should be compensated for them. Moreover, there was the additional problem of how to value the slots. At the time, the EU competition authorities were convinced that the incumbent carriers had no legal claim to the slots they held; the airlines, for their part, were equally convinced that they owned the slots.

---

11   Keith Boyfield, 'Don't Ground Competition over Airport Slots', *Wall Street Journal Europe*, 30 September 1997.

The outcome was a two-year stalemate ended only in July 1999 when the US Department of Transportation ruled that the alliance partners' application for immunity from anti-trust proceedings should be declined. This decision was, in part, made on the basis of the continued disagreements between BA and the competition authorities in the UK and Brussels, as well as the lack of progress achieved between the US and British governments on revising the present bilateral air service agreement.

Slots: who owns them?

Uncertainty over the definition of property rights as they relate to slots at congested airports remains a key feature of the civil aviation industry within the EU. Three separate parties lay claim to these property rights: the state, airport operators and airlines. In recent years all three aspirants have promoted their claims.

During the negotiations over whether BA should surrender slots at Heathrow and Gatwick in order to gain regulatory approval for its proposed alliance with American Airlines, John Prescott, the Deputy Prime Minister who held overall responsibility for transport issues, argued that airlines did not own the slots they held at congested airports. In an interview on BBC Radio 4's *World at One* on 11 August 1998, he observed, 'I have always been clear in my mind: the slots don't belong to BA. The slots belong, I believe, to the community.' He added that he was opposed to the secondary trading of slots. Indeed, he highlighted the fact that 'In my first months in office I made absolutely clear to the [regulatory] authorities that I did not think that was right.'

Sir Malcolm Rifkind, a Tory predecessor as Secretary of State for Transport, concurred with this view. In 1992 he told a parliamentary select committee that 'no airline has a legal right to a landing or take-off slot. Rather, airlines have permission and this must be subject to the public interest.'[12]

'The state', Robin Pratt of PriceWaterhouseCoopers has explained, 'could regard the redefined slots as licences to use a particular part of its airspace (just above the runway) at a particular time, on defined conditions. The state could hence issue (tradable) slot licences for a fee, representing the economic rent of the nonrenewable resource concerned.'[13] He cites as a parallel the example of government-issued oil production licences in the UK.

A second option would be to authorise airport operators to issue slot licences that airlines could trade on a secondary market. Not surprisingly, independent airport operators such as Richard Gooding, chief executive of London City Airport, strongly support the idea that property rights relating to slots should properly remain with the creator of the runway space.

This argument is supported by other leading figures in the civil aviation industry. Stelios Haji-Ioannou, the founder of EasyJet, champions the case for airport operators to assign slots in the form of tradable property rights. In an interview[14] with the author he pointed out, 'I think you have to allow market forces to work. There is nothing worse than grandfather rights. You have to think what creates a slot. A slot is really forty-seven seconds of a runway plus the associated use of taxiways, apron space to park the aircraft and terminal facilities. You therefore have to reach the

---

12   Parliamentary Select Committee on Transport, oral evidence, 15 May 1992, in response to Q847 by Mr Fry.
13   'The potential impact of slot trading on airport capacity management', conference paper given by Robin Pratt on 12 February 1998.
14   Held on 28 October 1997.

conclusion that the slot belongs to whoever built the runway in the first place. In my view the owner of the airport should be the owner of the slot, unless they decide to sell or lease a slot to an airline. Then you get market forces competing for more attractive slots and less attractive slots. If you really think you can make a fortune flying top executives to Tokyo for five thousand pounds a time, then you can afford to pay more for your slots at Heathrow.' The main shareholder in EasyJet added, 'That would benefit me in the following way: it would make sure that congested airports are properly priced.'

If new legislation were introduced which conferred the right to issue slot licences on the airports themselves, this would in effect amount to slots being treated as an extension of the operating rights already agreed between carriers and airport operators, for which the latter receive a fee by way of landing charges.

Interestingly, BAA has shied away from claiming slot ownership at its own airports, including the three major facilities it operates in the Greater London catchment area. The suspicion must be that this self-denying ordinance is linked to a fear that it would reopen a debate about its dominant monopoly of London airports. As Tom Bass observes, 'why should airport shareholders make a windfall profit from scarce supply? The airports cannot reasonably expect to reap this reward, particularly where they are subject to price regulation specifically to prevent abuse of their dominant position' (see page 91).

Yet as Stelios Haji-Ioannou points out, the merit of allowing airports to issue slot licences is that one allows market forces to operate. Adopting such a policy option would be a spur to optimising charging and capacity expansion. Indeed, the full value of scarce slots could be reflected in differentiated charges that would reduce the premiums paid on a secondary market. The charges generated from slot licences would provide a very useful signal to both airport operators and carriers as to the need for future investment in runway and terminal capacity. As Robin Pratt of PriceWaterhouseCoopers notes, 'In principle, such expansion should occur whenever the costs (including environmental costs) of doing so are lower than the costs of continuing with the congestion concerned.' The price mechanism would thus emerge for the first time in the UK as a capacity management tool which airport management could employ to meet demand. The question of BAA's dominant monopoly in the South-East is a separate factor that might be remedied through the disaggregation of its ownership of all three main airports (see later discussion).

The third option would be to allow airlines to hold slots outright. Airlines commonly argue that they need to be able to hold slots at busy airports in order to attract finance to maintain a modern, safe and attractive fleet of aircraft. It is also suggested that, in order to be profitable, an airline needs an assurance that it will be able to retain sufficient slots to maintain a viable scheduled service on a specific route. Otherwise it is claimed that those airlines that have the foresight and courage to invest in building services from under-used airports would lose the benefits of their investment to new entrants who have not had to share the cost and uncertainty of developing the airport. It therefore comes as no surprise to discover that national flag carriers are implacably opposed to the idea of primary trading of slots.

Bob Ayling, the former chief executive of BA, was never in any doubt that airlines should be able to claim airport slots as their property right. In negotiations over the BA/American Airlines alliance he was convinced that full compensation must be paid for any surrender of slots at Heathrow or Gatwick. Yet it is worth noting that in the US the Federal Aviation Administration's (FAA's) rules relating to secondary trading of slots at the four busiest airports specifically state that 'slots do not represent a property right but represent an operating privilege subject to absolute FAA control. Slots may be withdrawn at any time to fulfil the Department's operational needs.'[15]

The International Air Transport Association (IATA), the airlines' international trade association, has long employed a set of guidelines that rest on the principle of grandfather rights (i.e. if a carrier operated a slot in the equivalent season of the preceding year it is automatically renewed so long as the airline has been using the slot). For anti-trust reasons, the US government refuses to recognise these guidelines. But in the EU the European Commission used these guidelines as the basis of its directive 95/93. Tom Bass observes that 'Member States were anxious to preserve the continuity and practical efficiency of the IATA system and were unwilling to dilute grandfather rights' (see page 81).

The IATA guidelines are strongly supported by the incumbent airlines that happen to hold slots at the world's most congested airports. Yet recent entrants into the airline industry, who do not enjoy the status of national flag carriers, dispute this view. The kernel of Barry Humphreys' argument is that grandfather rights militate against new entry at congested airports and seriously constrain competition. At the time of the original negotiations over slot rules most European flag carriers were also state owned.

---

15   See Sec 93.223, cited in William H. Riker and Itai Sened, 'A Political Theory of the Origin of Property Rights: Airport Slots', in Lee J. Alston, Thrainn Eggertsson and Douglas C. North (eds), *Empirical Studies in Institutional Change*, Cambridge University Press, 1996.

Member State governments had little incentive to dilute the value of carriers, several of which have been subsequently privatised. What is more, airlines never paid anything for the slots in the first place. They do not appear on their balance sheets, nor did they feature in any privatisation prospectus.

The EU slot allocation directive (Council Regulation No. 95/93)

The EU has adopted the IATA guidelines for common EU purposes under the European Commission's Council Regulation No. 95/93. Yet this regulation has come to be seen as increasingly antiquated since it is based on the grandfathering rights of incumbent airlines. Carriers have little incentive to hand back slots they hold at peak times, no matter how inefficiently they are used.

Interpretations of the present EU directive differ markedly, depending on the vested interests of the interpreter. Chris Castles, who was a partner at the consulting firm PriceWaterhouseCoopers, has pointed out that the EU's objectives with regard to regulation 95/93 were 'open to various interpretations, and in practice there appears to be a range of views among Member States both on the form and extent to which competition should be promoted, and on the way in which competition and the efficient use of capacity should be reconciled'. In practice, individual airports have tended to implement the directive in the way that suits them. As those present at drafting meetings of regulation 95/93 have testified to the author, the slot allocation rules were drafted in a deliberately ambiguous fashion, so that the rules meant different things to different people.

For example, the present directive states that 'slots may be freely exchanged between air carriers or transferred by an air carrier from one route, or type of service, to another, by mutual agreement or as a result of a total or partial takeover or unilaterally'.[16] A number of conditions were placed on the ability of carriers to undertake any such exchanges or transfers, notably that such exchanges should be transparent and should not contravene the 'use it or lose it' provisions under Article 10 of the EC regulation. However, what does the phrase 'freely exchanged' mean in practice?

The Guernsey Transport Board case

The confusion surrounding this phrase prompted the States of Guernsey Transport Board to challenge in the British High Court KLM's legal right to sell slots it held at Heathrow in 1998 to BA. The Guernsey authorities were enraged by this sale because KLM's subsidiary, Air UK, had previously used eight daily slots to operate a scheduled service between Guernsey and Heathrow, Europe's most important hub airport which linked Guernsey to other major financial centres. Based on information published in KLM's annual report and accounts, the airline may have received up to 48 million guilders by way of financial compensation for the transfer of these prime slots at Heathrow.[17]

Lawyers in the case spent a great deal of time arguing about the precise legal meaning of slots being 'freely exchanged'. One group of lawyers argued that this phrase meant without hindrance, whilst the opposing side argued that it effectively meant that slot exchanges could not be accompanied by financial compensation.

---

16 See Article 8.

17 *Flight International* magazine reported that BA paid more than £2 million to KLM for each of these slots at Heathrow. See the *Guardian*, 9 July 1998.

The judge, Mr Justice Maurice Kay, ruled that slots at Heathrow could be exchanged freely for money and that the EU's Regulation 95/93 'embraced the transactions between Air UK and BA'. He noted that he had reached his decision 'on what I believe to be the clear meaning of the relevant words in the [EU] Regulation 95/93'.[18]

The British High Court decision, announced in March 1999, recognises that a secondary market in slots exists and effectively approves the right of airlines to exchange these scarce slots for money.[19] The Guernsey authorities have not pursued an appeal against the judge's decision. But this legal ruling reinforces the urgent need for the Council of Ministers to rethink the EC regulation on slot allocation, a review which is now several years overdue.

Proposals to revise the existing EU slot directive

The European Commission has spent at least five years of tortuous debate and negotiation seeking to agree a revised slot allocation directive. Initial attempts at hammering out a revised directive floundered because of disagreement within the Commission.

Karel van Miert was convinced that airlines had no legal claim

---

18 *Regina v. Airport Co-ordination Ltd exparte [CHECK]The States of Guernsey Transport Board*, High Court of Justice, Queen's Bench Division, 25 March 1999.

19 As *The Times* commented, the High Court decision effectively meant that BA enjoyed a windfall gain of £3 billion since it held over 3,200 weekly slots at Heathrow and a further 1,460 at slot-constrained Gatwick. However, airline share prices were not noticeably affected by the High Court ruling, suggesting that investors had already priced the value of slots held at congested airports into the overall share price. Chris Tarry, a leading airline analyst, formerly with Commerzbank Securities, supports this view, pointing out that without slots, airlines do not have a business.

on slots while Neil Kinnock was keen to recognise the grey market in the secondary trading of slots, which has gone on for many years.

It was only after a new crop of Commissioners was appointed that significant progress was made. In 2000, Loyola de Palacio, the vice-president responsible for transport and energy, sought to introduce new proposals allowing for partial auctioning of slots and secondary trading of slots. This proposal was effectively vetoed by Member States and by a lobbying campaign adopted by European flag carriers who enjoyed grandfathering rights at congested airports. It was agreed that the Commission should work on an interim revision of the EU slot directive, which would take account of developments within the airline industry. However, slot trading and auctioning was specifically excluded from this draft proposal, pending more detailed research.

A year later, the Commission published its draft revision proposals, and these were debated in a First Reading by the European Parliament in June 2002. In a show of hands, there was overwhelming support for the new legislation, although certain modifications were suggested. This revised proposal designates slots as government-controlled concessions, not the property of airlines or airports.

The modified proposals were sent to the Council of Ministers in autumn 2002. As yet, transport ministers have not had an opportunity to discuss these revisions. Under the Greek presidency of the EU, such a discussion may take place in the spring or early summer of 2003. However, the process may be further delayed because the Commission has appointed the economic consultants NERA (National Economic Research Associates) to submit a detailed study of the effects of different slot allocation systems by July 2003. This study[20] will seek to quantify and identify the respective costs and benefits of the various possible slot allocation options, including auctions and secondary trading. NERA has also been asked to illustrate possible combinatorial approaches in a series of matrices.

In practice, the European Commission is unlikely to gain approval for any revision of the existing slot allocation rules before 2004. Some relatively minor technical revisions may be implemented in late 2003 as a result of the existing modified proposals submitted by the Commission. But any more radical revision of the slot allocation rules is unlikely to win the necessary political approval before spring 2004 at the earliest.

Britain is one of the Member States that is in favour of adopting a more market-oriented approach to the allocation of slots at congested airports. Such an approach would also allow for an open, transparent market in the secondary trading of slots. The Civil Aviation Authority (CAA) has consistently supported such an initiative and has published its own views in two detailed studies.[21] Treasury officials are also in favour of such a radical overhaul to the allocation of slots. The Treasury's viewpoint is not entirely altruistic, since it senses that it can levy a windfall tax on revenue generated by such slot sales.

---

20 NERA is undertaking this study, following a competitive tender, in collaboration with the Institute of Aviation Law at the University of Leiden in the Netherlands.

21 See, for example, *The Implementation of Secondary Slot Trading*, CAA, November 2001.

A recommended way forward: adopt a market approach

The lacuna that presently bedevils the issue of slots at congested airports could be resolved by adopting market mechanisms. Airlines' access to slots at congested airports can make the difference between financial success and bankruptcy. Indeed, when airlines have filed for bankruptcy, as with PanAm and TWA, their slots at airports like Heathrow are often their most valuable asset.

There is a pressing need for new legislation to define property rights as they relate to slots. Such legislation should define the nature of the slot, the rights and obligations that go with holding them, as well as the rules on primary and secondary trading of these scarce resources at congested airports. The present administrative rules for allocating scarce capacity at congested airports are clearly inefficient in terms of awarding such capacity to the highest-value use. There also appears to be an arbitrary distinction drawn between new entrants and long-established incumbents associated with the lack of clarity about overall policy objectives.

In this context, markets have a valuable role to perform in providing transparency and flexibility. Airports should have the primary claim on property rights as they relate to slots. After all, they create the capacity in the first place. At the same time, it must be acknowledged that they are granted this right by the government, which issues planning permission to create the slots at airports, most notably in the crowded South-East of England. In authorising new runway capacity it is therefore legitimate for the government to levy a tax on behalf of the community to address the externality costs which airports generate. Such a tax should be levied in the form of a licence collected from existing airport operators as well as from potential new suppliers of runway, terminal and related facilities.

Airport operators should then be free to set market-related prices for the slots they offer to airlines. A slot would comprise the right to use a runway for a landing or take-off, and the associated stand, apron space and share of terminal capacity that go with such use. Slot prices should be determined by market demand with premium rates applying at peak periods. The preferred method would be a system based on auctioning slots, with carriers bidding for convenient slots to suit their preferred timetable of operations. On behalf of the UK government, DotEcon Ltd, a firm of economic consultants, has undertaken some detailed analysis of how this might be done in practice, employing simultaneous multiple-round auctions (SMRAs).[22]

In setting out a range of potential auction designs for the primary allocation of airport slots, DotEcon Ltd argues that 'despite the complexity of allocating runway slots, there are workable auction designs that could yield significant benefits compared with existing procedures'. The economic consultants point out that adaptations of auction formats employed to allocate radio spectrum provide a feasible method of allocating airport slots. In any auction process, the right to exercise a slot should be strictly time-limited, since it is important to have a significant proportion of slots that are available through the primary auction process. This promotes competition and enables new entrants and smaller carriers to bid for slots at the more congested airports.

---

22 *Auctioning Airport Slots*, a report for HM Treasury and the Department of the Environment, Transport and the Regions, DotEcon Ltd, January 2001.

Where it is judged appropriate to safeguard certain services to regional cities throughout the UK – for example, to Belfast, which is separated by the Irish Sea from the UK mainland – the regulatory authorities could reserve slots or use subsidies to maintain services. A more efficient economic option might be to encourage local authorities or regional governments to buy slots at congested airports, such as Heathrow and Gatwick, or bid in partnership with airlines seeking to provide shuttle services to and from London. Such an option would meet public interest objectives yet, at the same time, keep economic distortions to a minimum since slots would have to be acquired at the going market rate.

Inevitably, any proposed auction system is likely to exhibit certain flaws. Accordingly, there is a role for a secondary market that enables carriers to exchange slots. At any one time, some slots will be worth more to one airline than to another, so it is to be expected that money will change hands (and even if it does not, carriers will barter other non-monetised forms of benefit with one another). However, the secondary market should not give rise to excessive premiums if the auction system is performing its function properly in matching demand with supply.

The demand for slots at congested airports will give a good indication of the need to build new capacity, whether in the form of incremental additions, such as new apron space and terminal capacity, or in the form of major new facilities, such as the construction of new runways or feeder-reliever satellites.

These proposals are based on a strategy for an ideal world. But the world is far from ideal, particularly in the South-East of England. Incumbent airlines would immediately object to the proposals just outlined because they represent a direct attack on their commercial interests. Yet, it can be argued, the aversion of incumbent carriers to auction systems is a reflection of the fact that they want to be granted the property rights relating to scarce slots while not having to compensate those who grant those rights. Nonetheless, if there were to be any chance of implementing an auction-based system of slot allocation, it would be necessary to phase in over time such a radical market-oriented approach. Furthermore, it must be accepted that new legislation would need to be introduced on an EU-wide basis, since the allocation of slots at congested 'Community airports' is governed by common rules. Member States' potential opposition to a more market-oriented approach with regard to the allocation of slots cannot be underestimated. Likewise, incumbent carriers at congested airports will almost certainly challenge the legal basis of any new EU-wide legislation through the courts.

Bearing in mind these considerations, Barry Humphreys' suggestion that each year a random batch of 10 per cent of the available slots at London's three main airports should be offered on ten- or fifteen-year franchises appears attractive. Over ten years all the available slots will come up for auction to the carriers who find them most valuable. But by phasing in this radical new approach, airlines' past investment and value added through the development of new routes would be recognised. And, as Barry Humphreys argues, any carrier that is unable to generate a return on a route within ten years should not be flying the route. Alternatively, the route should be operated by a more efficient airline.

Possible objections

Critics will advance a wide range of arguments as to why such a radical departure should be opposed. However, in the author's judgement none of them is sufficiently compelling to abrogate a move towards such a market-oriented initiative. Let us consider these tricky hurdles in turn.

The monopoly rent problem

It will be objected that BAA, the operator of all three main airports in the South-East, should not be entitled to extract a monopoly rent for slots at Heathrow and Gatwick, which are both seriously congested. This objection can be addressed in three ways.

First, as already outlined, by collecting a levy on the windfall profits generated from scarce slots at London's principal airports, the government could tackle associated environmental problems such as noise and surface access as well as appraise new capacity options.

Second, BAA as a monopoly could be broken up on the assumption that competing companies would strive to attract carriers to their airports in a number of innovative ways. As a consequence, traffic patterns might alter markedly. Competing airport companies are likely to be more enthusiastic supporters of new initiatives such as the development of feeder-reliever airports at under-utilised aerodromes such as Northolt, close to Heathrow, and Redhill, five miles north of Gatwick.[23] Competing airport companies and new entrants might also explore radical new options such as the development of a major new hub at Cliffe

---

23   The author has detailed the arguments in favour of such a policy option in *Plane Commonsense*, published by the Adam Smith Institute, and in written and oral evidence to the select committee on transport; see *Regional Air Services*, 8th report, July 1998, and minutes of evidence, Stationery Office, 3 June 1998.

on the Hoo Peninsula in North Kent,[24] or the development of a new airport and runways on an artificial island in the Thames estuary. (This latter suggestion is not such a fanciful concept: a major international airport was opened at Kansai, two and a half miles offshore from Osaka in Japan, in 1994; and a similar concept has been considered by Schiphol airport in the Netherlands.[25])

Market clearing prices would be inflationary and damaging to consumer interests

It can be argued that Heathrow is such a popular international hub that the market clearing price would have to be very high in order to divert traffic to other airports in the South-East. Furthermore, consumers may well fear that they will have to pay far more to use Heathrow. In response it can be observed that the elasticity of demand for slots at Heathrow has never been tested. Nevertheless, the elasticity of demand might result in some very high premiums being paid, as implied in the findings of the RUCATSE report. But consumers should not necessarily need to pay higher fares since airlines are presently benefiting from a transfer in economic rent from the airport operator, BAA, which is unable to charge the market clearing price for regulatory reasons. Incumbent carriers are simply charging what the market will bear.

Slots priced according to airline demand would channel income directly to the creator of the airport facilities. From

---

24 The reasons for selecting the Cliffe site are detailed in *The Future Development of Air Transport in the United Kingdon: South East,* a consultation document published by the Department of Transport, July 2002.

25 This would involve constructing an artificial island offshore in the North Sea.

WHO OWNS AIRPORT SLOTS?

this revenue stream the government might levy a tax based on licensing airport development. Additionally, it must be pointed out that charging the market-related price for scarce slots would promote the attractiveness of under-utilised secondary airports such as Stansted, Luton, Southampton and Southend.

The adoption of auctions and secondary trading markets could lead to predation and anti-competitive behaviour by dominant airlines

Another argument likely to be deployed is that a slot allocation system based on auctions would be dominated by the major airlines, which might well be motivated to buy up slots to exclude new entrants. But as David Starkie points out, academic research in the US on the experience of secondary trading at airports suggests that this is an extremely expensive way for established airlines to drive out rival carriers. And, as the Consumers' Association has pointed out, 'no matter how deep the pockets of any airline, it is unlikely that it would be able to buy up all slots, nor bid in more slots than it could afford to operate. It is hardly likely that the financiers of airlines would allow this to occur.'[26]

Any tendency towards anti-competitive practices by individual airlines or airline alliances can, of course, be tackled through the application of existing competition law. As the CAA has argued, 'European and UK competition laws, the UK Fair Trading Act and merger regimes all provide possible avenues to guard against the holding and possible anti-competitive effect of a dominant

26 *Airline Competition – a long haul for the consumer*, policy report published by the Consumers' Association, 1997, p. 52. See also McGowan and Seabright's study on 'Deregulating European Airlines', *Economic Policy*, October 1989, pp. 283–344.

position in a slot or related market.'[27] Furthermore, such is the financial fragility of many traditional carriers following the 11 September 2001 atrocities in the US that few of them have sufficiently deep pockets to hoard slots.

The Chicago Convention

In any discussion of the economics of airports the Chicago Convention, signed in December 1944, is often cited as an international treaty that precludes airports from charging fees that reflect market demand. On closer scrutiny, it can be seen that the relevant article[28] of the Convention is essentially concerned with maintaining a non-discriminatory regime. It provides that 'every airport in a contracting state which is open to public use by its national aircraft shall likewise ... be open under uniform conditions to the aircraft of all the other contracting states'. The Convention further stipulates that any charge imposed by a state for the use of such airports or of its air navigation facilities by the aircraft of any other contracting state shall not be higher than that paid by its national aircraft engaged in similar international services or similar operations.

This point again relates to non-discrimination but it may be cited by airlines that feel disgruntled about paying slot fees. If an attempt were made to employ the Chicago Convention as a block to prevent a more market-oriented system of slot allocation this might well spur calls for a thorough review of the Convention itself. After all, the treaty was signed almost sixty years ago, when

---

27   *The Implementation of Secondary Slot Trading*, CAA, November 2001, p. iv.
28   Article 15.

there was scarcely any risk of airport congestion. Fifty-nine years after it was drawn up, it may now be time to revise the Chicago Convention to bring it into line with the more competitive airline industry we see today. Such a move would also complement the drive by both the US and UK governments towards an 'open skies' aviation policy. After all, overcrowded airports are one of the main barriers to the achievement of this goal.

Bilateral air service agreements (ASAs)

Ian Jones and Ivan Viehoff of NERA, two economists who advocate greater use of market mechanisms and slot trading, acknowledge that 'a large proportion of scheduled international air services between the UK and non-EU countries will be the subject of restrictive agreements with overseas governments, which carry with them an obligation on the part of the UK government to ensure that airport capacity is available to operate the service'.[29]

The most important bilateral ASA impinging on London's airports is that between the UK and the US, often referred to as Bermuda 2. This states that user charges should be 'just and reasonable for this purpose'. The crucial question to be answered is what constitutes a reasonable profit margin?

Adopting a market approach, and given the availability of substitute airports, it could be argued that charges should be raised to reflect market demand. Airlines which judge that slot prices are too high could switch to other airports in the Greater London area. However, the advantage of an auction-based system is that any airline would be able to bid for slots, enabling

---

29   See *The Economics of Airport Slots*, NERA Topics, January 1993.

much greater competition on popular routes such as services between London and major American cities. As matters currently stand, the bilateral ASA between the UK and US allows only two US carriers and two British carriers to operate transatlantic flights from Heathrow. These restrictions have led to a sustained lobbying campaign by airlines seeking to promote or defend their commercial interests – and publicly quoted share price.[30]

Some commentators[31] argue that bilaterals would make it extremely difficult to move to a slot allocation system based on auctions. This is because existing bilateral ASAs are founded on the principle of grandfathering rights, as recognised by IATA guidelines and the current EC Regulation 95/93. ASAs consequently represent a system of regulatory intervention which has tended to shackle market mechanisms; bilaterals tend to be highly restrictive. Indeed, they have been one of the principal factors underpinning the inefficient system of administrative slot allocation that remains in force at Heathrow and Gatwick today.

The aim must be to renegotiate ASAs on the basis that scarce slots at congested UK airports will be auctioned off with an open, transparent secondary trading market available to airlines that find it convenient to exchange slots. Such a secondary market would be administered by the airport coordinator and regulated by the CAA. On practical political grounds it may, of course, be necessary to restrict trading mechanisms initially to EU routes while bilateral ASAs are renegotiated. In the longer term, the objective would be to build international support for a market-based auction system of allocating slots at congested airports, as part of

---

30   See, for example, 'BA seeks to protect its routes over the Atlantic', *Financial Times*, 27 January 2000.

31   For example, the NERA Topic paper op cit stresses this point.

a liberalised, open skies regime throughout North America and Europe. In this context, it is encouraging to learn that the CAA would ideally prefer to abolish bilaterals in favour of an open skies approach encompassing a wider and fully liberalised common aviation area.

One final problem

Returning to the question of who should receive the income generated by market-related slot tariffs, it can be argued that there is a real danger that the government might be tempted to restrict new capacity on the grounds that this will allow the Treasury to optimise the revenues collected from slot licences at existing airports, principally Heathrow and Gatwick. This must be recognised as a major problem, but one that in principle can be addressed by an economic regulator.

The workings of the market should help to assign slots to those airlines that find them most valuable. Furthermore, if BAA's monopoly is broken up, one might well find that rival operators would do more to maximise the efficient use of existing capacity. After all, it must be noted that BAA has failed to build any new runways in the South-East since it was privatised. And if slot charges were perceived as being excessively high, surely this would be the market signal that new capacity, whether in the form of feeder-relievers, new runways or new airports, should be constructed.

The high price of slots could then be channelled into reducing the noise impact of airports and reducing road traffic congestion. Adopting such a policy approach would be the most appropriate way of addressing local residents' resistance to the expansion of airports in the UK economy.[32] It would also help to shape the general public's attitude – and, for that matter, their political representatives' attitude – to the role of civil aviation in a modern society. If people want to continue to be able to take advantage of the low-cost airlines such as Ryanair and EasyJet, which have emerged in the aftermath of the liberalisation of European air services, they must have airports from which to operate.

---

32 For an overview of the economic importance of airports in the UK economy, see *The Contribution of the Aviation Industry to the UK Economy*, Oxford Economic Forecasting, November 1999. See also the first chapter in *Plane Commonsense: the case for feeder-reliever airports in the South East* by Keith Boyfield, Adam Smith Institute, 1994.

2 THE ECONOMICS OF SECONDARY MARKETS FOR AIRPORT SLOTS
David Starkie[1]

Introduction

The current downturn in world aviation markets has eased pressures on capacity at a number of major airports, but in many cases capacity shortages continue to exist. There are a number of reasons for this. The overwhelming majority of airports are still publicly controlled utilities subject to political whims and tight budgets, but even where such constraints apply less (as in the UK) expansion has been hampered by environmental limitations and other planning controls. Building new runways or lengthening existing ones is not always an easy task.

As a consequence, expansion of air services has had to rely increasingly upon improvements in air traffic control technology and the adoption of new procedures to squeeze more aircraft movements through existing facilities. The ability to do so has been at times remarkable. Thirty years ago, the Roskill Commission investigating locations suitable for a new international airport for London adopted the working assumption that the estimated capacity of Heathrow and Gatwick combined was 440,000 annual air traffic movements: in 2000 Heathrow *alone* handled 460,000 air traffic movements. Nor has the process of improving

---

1   This paper copyright David Starkie.

throughput slackened in recent times. Nevertheless, the salient feature remains one of shortages of capacity; at many major airports runways are operating at, or close to, declared capacity for some or much of the day,[2] and the allocation of this scarce capacity has become a major issue.

Two approaches predominate for its allocation. For much of the world outside the US the basic approach is to allocate capacity according to a set of rules based on guidelines laid down by IATA, the airline trade association. These guidelines, first and foremost, recognise the historical use of 'slots' (the entitlement to use a runway on a particular day at a particular time, usually expressed in fifteen-minute blocks). An airline has a right to a slot if it has already made use of the runway at the same time during the preceding equivalent season. These entitlements, commonly known as 'grandfathered rights', form the point of reference at biannual international conferences that take place to coordinate schedules at capacity-restricted airports. At these conferences, airlines seek to modify their schedules by exchanging (transferring) between themselves their existing slot holdings, or perhaps by trying to obtain additional slots that occasionally become available (although since 1990 the IATA rules have required a proportion of available slots to be set aside for use by new-entrant carriers, defined as those with negligible or non-existent presence at the airport concerned). These basic guidelines were adopted into EU law, albeit

---

2   Declared capacity and its composition are determined not only by the runway constraints at an airport but also by the limitations of stand and terminal capacity. Even if one of the latter is the overriding constraint this will be reflected in the capacity declaration for the runway. To simplify the argument in the rest of the paper, we will focus on the runway constraint. For a good account of the interactions between the different components of airport capacity, see Turvey (2000).

with some minor changes, by Regulation 95/93 early in 1993. The regulation is currently subject to review.

In contrast, in the US, for anti-trust reasons, the IATA-based system does not apply. Airlines cannot meet to discuss schedules, routes, services, nor, of course, fares. Partly because of this, there are few restrictions at US airports limiting the allocation of landing and take-off slots; for example, airline scheduling committees, which have an important slot management role outside the USA, do not operate at US airports. Airlines simply schedule their flights taking into account expected delays at the busier airports. Essentially, slots are allocated on a first come, first served basis, with the length of the queue of planes waiting to land or take-off acting to ration overall demand. Although this is the general situation in the US there is an important exception; at a small number of busy airports where the FAA prescribes the hourly number of flight operations, departure and arrival slots can be bought and sold (traded) in a secondary market. This exception is significant because it substitutes for rationing by queue or by administrative rule a market-based approach to slot allocation.

In the next section, we review the allocation of scarce airport capacity in relation to economic principles, concluding that a secondary market has the potential to achieve an efficient allocation. This is followed by a consideration of a number of specific issues relating to the operations of a secondary market for airport slots. These issues include whether structural differences between markets and in the technology of supply will lead to an inefficient allocation of slots in a secondary market; whether incumbent airlines will use a secondary market to engage in predatory bidding; whether efficiency factors can be expected to lead to a concentration of slot holdings; and whether slot concentration might result in a reduction in the external costs of delay and thus produce a positive externality. The subsequent two sections consider the workings of the US slot markets and examine the hypothesis that dominant carriers might have made less efficient use of slots acquired in the secondary markets. This is followed by a penultimate section, which draws together the strands of the various arguments and also considers their public policy implications.

Optimal allocation

Neither the approach commonly used in the US nor that commonly used in the rest of the world to allocate slots at capacity-constrained airports conforms to an economically efficient approach. An economically efficient approach would allocate scarce capacity by basing a charge for the use of runways on the marginal cost of use. The *de minimus* marginal cost is the additional wear and tear caused to the runway/taxiway infrastructure by the extra aircraft movement (with other airfield costs such as fire and rescue cover, unaffected by the marginal movement). This cost is only weakly related to pavement strength and the weight of the aircraft because of other factors relating to the design of the aircraft and its landing gear; nevertheless, damage costs can be calculated with reasonable accuracy and are aircraft-type specific (Hogan, Feighan and Starkie, 2002). At congested airports, however, the significant marginal cost is the cost associated with the delay that a flight by one airline imposes on other airlines' flights. Delay increases fuel burn, reduces the productivity of aircraft assets and staff and is a cost to passengers because increased travel time has negative value. These losses are accentuated by the uncertainty associated with the delays; both airlines and passengers schedule to allow for above-average delays. To achieve an economically efficient use of slots, such externalities need to be incorporated in the user charge and added to the charge reflecting the damage caused to runway pavements by the additional aircraft movement.

Marginal cost pricing of runway use (and thus the allocation of slots by price alone) does not exist in world aviation, at least not in the precise form outlined. There are a few congested airports that make some distinction between charges for peak and off-peak use (in the form of surcharges or discounts on a standard charge) but these are typically superimposed on an aircraft weight-based tariff structure. The absence of a more efficient charging structure is partly because of the complexities of calculating a robust charge based on marginal costs. But the chief reason is the conservatism of airport authorities and especially the strong opposition of airlines to the idea of using the price mechanism for allocation purposes. At busy airports used by many different airlines, the effect of marginal cost pricing would be to increase peak charges, probably substantially, and thus reduce the scarcity rents or abnormal returns that incumbent airlines using runways at peak times obtain from their access to a scarce resource at a nominal tariff.[3] It would also have the effect of transferring the scarcity rents to airport companies, leading in turn to issues of whether, for these companies, returns on capital were excessive.

There is, however, an approach that has the potential to square the circle. This is to allow incumbent airlines to retain their rights to slots already held under the grandfathering rule but also to allow them to sell these rights to non-incumbents, or to buy

---

3   At off-peak times, marginal cost-based tariffs would probably *decrease* from current (average cost) levels.

further slots themselves, in a secondary market. The secondary market would provide an opportunity for an efficient allocation of slots to evolve, and thus eliminate the allocative inefficiencies that result from price controls and administrative rationing. In the process, slots would be transferred to those airlines that can use them to add most value to the service network. It would enable high-added-value users of runway capacity to compensate, through the purchase price, users with low added value. By allowing the market to redistribute slots to services from which airline passengers derive most benefit there would be a net gain in welfare.[4] It is also quite possible that the average fare yield would increase as a consequence. Because scarce capacity would now be utilised by flights from which passengers derive most benefit, airlines would be able to extract an additional economic rent in higher fares.

The introduction of a secondary market in airline slots will mean, of course, that the incumbent slot holder receives a lump-sum financial benefit when a slot is purchased either by another incumbent or by an entrant, and this financial transfer might be considered to give incumbents an undue advantage. But this lump sum represents the present value of the scarcity rent associated with the slot. The incumbent is currently receiving this scarcity value through the yield premium on fares charged to passengers.[5]

---

4   A legitimate question is: why do those airlines with historic rights serving low-value markets not switch services to more highly valued markets? In other words, is not the division of the market portrayed here rather artificial? The division reflects both barriers to entry associated with international air service agreements and the absence of a market in slots; airlines do not have an incentive to earn a return on assets that are freely acquired and are not fully tradable.

5   Recent analysis by the CAA (2002: 14–18) suggests that for an airport like Heathrow the yield premium can be quite large.

In this respect those with grandfather rights already enjoy the 'windfall' and the introduction of a formal slot market will neither add to nor subtract from this.[6]

The potential for misallocating slots

The argument that a secondary market will secure an efficient allocation of slots assumes that airlines competing for slots are also competing in the market for passengers. Where this is not the case – where, for example, bilateral air service agreements restrict the frequency of service and number of carriers on a route – it could be argued that an optimal allocation of slots would not be the outcome of a secondary market. This is because market expansion by the route monopolist would lead to a fall in yields as lower prices are paid by existing as well as new traffic. An airline expanding to the same degree in a more competitive and thus price-elastic market would see yields eroded less. Consequently, the monopolist would be less interested in purchasing slots in a secondary market and might, instead, become a net seller of slots. The result could be too few slots used (and services provided) in less competitive markets relative to the more competitive markets.

In addition, it has also been argued that even when there are no administrative restrictions on market entry – for example, in intra-EU markets or in the US domestic market – a secondary market for slots will not necessarily secure their most efficient use (Borenstein, 1988). Borenstein has argued that the use of a slot in any particular market is driven by the opportunities for profit, but there can be a poor correlation between the amount of profit and

6   See Starkie and Thompson (1985) for elaboration.

the amount of social surplus, and that this difference will vary from route to route. The difference will be a factor of the use of different production technologies by different firms (airlines), of the varying attributes of different markets in terms of demand elasticities, of the number of incumbent firms and of the opportunities for price discrimination.

In particular, it is argued that the equality of profits and social surplus, and hence equality between profits and efficiency, fails for two particular reasons. First, lumpiness in supply means that infra-marginal output produces consumer surplus that cannot be captured by the firm. And, second, entry onto routes with incumbent airlines will have the effect of transferring some rent from the incumbent(s) to the entrant; this transfer does not change the overall social surplus but, nevertheless, it accrues as profits to the entrant. This will cause the entrant to overvalue the licence (slot) and possibly lead to too much entry in crowded markets, and vice versa.

When Borenstein came to consider the airport slot market (his initial arguments were couched in the general context of licences to operate in restricted markets) he was, however, more sanguine. This was because the amount of capacity that could be provided by any single flight was limited, so that he acknowledged that capacity additions might be more welfare-enhancing in established airline markets than his earlier abstract analysis had supposed. Moreover, since Borenstein wrote his paper, technical developments have reduced the scale of the problems he raised. The introduction into service of regional jets has provided a technology that allows for smaller increments of supply. And improvements to and the spread of yield management techniques have enabled firms to finely tune prices in most aviation markets. These developments, in turn, increase the ability of all airlines to extract more surplus as profit and, therefore, the variation in demand elasticities across markets is likely to be less of a problem than Borenstein originally supposed.

By the same token, the ability that now exists to price-discriminate within the market in a sophisticated manner also reduces the likelihood that the route monopolist will restrict supply and thus be inclined to purchase fewer slots in a secondary market.[7] The importance of price discrimination is a point that we return to later in the paper.

Trading, predation and anti-competitive behaviour

A further argument, advanced in opposition to the view that a secondary market achieves an efficient distribution of slots, is that airlines will engage in predatory bidding for slots. Specifically, the argument is that established airlines with grandfathered rights might buy slots to keep entrants out of the market and, as a consequence, further increase their dominance at congested airports. This argument has been subject to close examination by

---

7   If this is considered to remain a significant problem it might be addressed in several ways. First, slots used on routes where entry is restricted by, for example, bilateral agreements could be ring-fenced and excluded from the processes of the secondary market, thus preventing the transfer of slots from less to more competitive markets. This is in effect the approach used in the US trading market, where trades are limited to slots used for domestic services. Second, additional slots that result from improvements in runway utilisation, or air traffic control procedures, could be restricted for use only on routes operated in a less competitive environment. Third, a differential tax with a higher rate applying to competitive routes could be introduced. The tax difference would equate to the mark-up of fares over airline operating costs on the monopoly routes. However, the information requirements for such an approach are demanding and air service agreements would probably prevent its implementation.

McGowan and Seabright (1989). They accept that it has substance but are of the view that, for established airlines, it is an expensive way to deter or drive out competitors. This is because at any one airport there are many slots, each one of which has a large number of close or reasonably close substitutes (bearing in mind that slots are transferable between services). To keep a newcomer out of a particular market, an incumbent airline might, therefore, have to 'overbid' on a large number of slots. In these circumstances, it is argued that it is more likely that an established airline will direct any predatory behaviour to the route (service) itself, where it will be more focused.

At an airport like Heathrow, where the largest airline (BA) and its alliance partners hold around 40 per cent of the slots overall and a similar proportion in the peak, this argument appears reasonable: attempts to keep potential entrants out of the market by overbidding on slots will be expensive and are unlikely to occur. But the McGowan and Seabright counter-argument is weaker at an airport such as Frankfurt, where over 60 per cent of slots are in the hands of Lufthansa, or Atlanta, where Delta's share exceeds 70 per cent. Here the number of slots on which these incumbents would need to overbid could be small. Consequently, at an airport where the incumbent already holds the majority of slots, overbidding might be a feasible way of preventing entry.[8]

There is a need, however, to take an additional factor into account. Once a formal secondary slot market is introduced at an

---

8   Wolf (1999) suggests that an airline could try to monopolise the slots by making a one-shot offer to current slot holders to buy all slots at a fixed and *ex ante* pre-specified price, with the offer terminating if there is not a complete acceptance. Of course, such a strategy would be conspicuous to the competition authorities and would probably fail on competition grounds.

airport, its slots become tradable assets and, as a result, their value should be written into the balance sheet of the airlines using the airport. This balance sheet value will reflect the market value of the slot, which in turn will reflect the capitalisation of the economic rent that the average airline can command from the use of a slot. Consequently, slots will be bought when an airline is able to earn a satisfactory return on the investment (because the purchaser judges that it will be able to extract more rents from the acquired slots than the airline selling the slots) and slots will be sold when their worth to an airline is less than their market (book) value.

In this context, overbidding the price of slots to remove competitors from the market, or to keep entrants out, could result in the acquisition of poorly performing assets, although this has to be balanced by the higher returns on other slots now subject to less competition. Where the balance will lie is not self-evident, but the complexity of the trade-offs involved suggests that predatory behaviour, should it take place, is more likely to focus on the level of fares set for routes subject to, or threatened with, entry.

Incentives for slot concentration

Although the concerns of the competition authorities have been driven by the prospect that trading could reinforce the position of large incumbent airlines at major airports, there are in fact a number of reasons why efficiency considerations might lead to a concentration of slots and to an increase in dominance at such locations. In large measure, incentives to concentrate slot holdings stem from the well-known economies associated with networks and the advantages of concentrating flows in networks on particular nodes referred to as hubs. The number of potential connections at a hub airport increases exponentially with the increase in the number of markets served from a hub; as a consequence there is a positive externality generated by concentrating flights. Potential travellers are faced with increasing opportunities to fly to and from their preferred end points, which increases the attractiveness of a hub airport as more and more cities are added to the network. In addition to these attractions of the scope of a hub network, the concentration of traffic at the hub allows for increased service frequencies along routes radiating from the hub. This increase in frequency enables passengers to match more closely their preferred time of travel with the scheduled time of the flight and thus to reduce schedule delay. These advantages to the passenger are not without some associated costs in the form of more circuitous and longer journeys but, overall, the passenger is considered to gain from airlines concentrating their flights by making an airport a hub (Morrison and Winston, 1986).

In addition to these demand-side benefits of network scope and density, there are potential supply-side gains from concentration. Concentration can generate cost efficiencies because of economies of route density (with fixed station costs, for example, spread over more units of output as a network of pre-determined size is used more intensely) and because of cost economies of network scale and scope (with larger networks enabling the better utilisation of aircraft fleets, for example).[9] The result of these scale economies, together with the demand synergies of networks, is

---

9   Ng and Seabright (2001), using a panel of twelve European and seven major US airlines for the period 1982–95, find returns to density of 1.19 and returns to scale of 1.09, although the indications were that returns to scale were exhausted at higher levels of output.

that a slot can be more valuable if it is used to enhance an existing network of services.

These demand-side economies, which encourage airlines to focus their operations at particular airports, do not in themselves predicate hub dominance. It is to be noted that the demand-side economics of the hub system could work equally well if every end point on the network was served from the hub by a different airline. Similarly, that part of the supply-side gain which comes from the economies of density could also in theory be realised if each route were served by a different airline. This is not true, however, in relation to the economies of network scale and scope: in a concentrated network these benefits accrue from airline concentration. In addition, studies have also shown that passengers have a preference for making on-line connections rather than transferring between airlines even where such transfers are formalised through IATA interline agreements.[10] This preference reinforces the attractiveness of the airline that happens to have the larger presence at the hub. In these circumstances, and in the absence of regulatory constraints, at major airports with limited capacity one might expect both consumer preferences and cost efficiencies to lead to an increasing concentration of slot holdings.[11]

Congestion externalities

The traditional approach to the measurement of congestion externalities assumes that the delay that one flight imposes on all other flights is a true measure of the external costs imposed by

---

10 See Economics-Plus and GRA (2000) for analysis of this effect. Available from GRA, 115 West Avenue, Jenkintown, PA 19046, USA.

11 These same factors encourage airline concentration (see Bailey and Liu, 1995).

that flight. But recent economics literature on the costs of airport congestion has argued that this approach overstates marginal costs (Brueckner, 2002; Mayer and Sinai, 2002). It does not take into account the fact that a particular flight might very well impose delay on other flights operated by the *same* airline, and that the delay costs that an airline imposes upon itself are, in effect, internalised and no longer constitute an externality. In these circumstances, treating the delay that each flight imposes on *all* other flights as a cost is only valid for airports where each and every flight is operated by a different airline. At the other extreme, an airport totally dominated by one airline cannot experience congestion externalities: congestion might exist but its level is of the monopolist's own choosing.

This argument has particular relevance at those airports chosen as hubs and at which dominant airlines concentrate their schedules into limited times of the day. At airline-dominant hub airports, the hub airline will seek to organise flight schedules into banks or waves of arriving flights mirrored by waves of departing flights with the intention of minimising passenger transfer times. Such concentration of flights into narrow windows of time increases the likelihood of congestion, as does the process of adding more end points to the network. But the passenger is gaining from reduced connection times and from the increasing reach of the network, so that longer delays are the outcome of a hub airline equating the high marginal benefits due to increasing concentration with the increasing marginal cost of delay, a decision process which internalises the externality in seeking to reach an efficient equilibrium (Mayer and Sinai, 2002).

One implication that follows from this view – that not all

delays constitute an external cost – is that an optimal congestion charge will vary depending not only on the amount of delay
that each additional flight imposes, but also on the proportion of
flights at an airport operated by each airline. Specifically, the appropriate charge is the delay cost imposed by the additional flight
multiplied by one minus each airline's share of total slot numbers
(Brueckner, 2002). Consequently, an additional flight by one airline with 50 per cent of the movements at an airport would pay
half the level of (congestion) charge paid by an equivalent flight
operated by a new-entrant airline.[12] Equally, if the largest airline
operating at a congested airport increased its slot holding from,
say, 50 to 55 per cent of the total, the congestion charge paid by its
flights should fall by 10 per cent, enabling the airline to capture
the internalisation of the delay externality in reduced charges.
Thus, if slot concentration reduces the delay externality this benefit from slot concentration should be reflected in prices charged.
Of course, as we have noted, efficient pricing of delay is difficult
to achieve (hence the current focus on secondary markets). Thus,
given the constraints on setting optimal prices, the appropriate
response is to pay a Pigouvian subsidy; the airline acquiring slots
in the secondary market should receive a subsidy equivalent to the
reduction in the delay externality.

---

12 Note that this outcome depends upon a stable and recurrent daily pattern of
flights. If, in contrast, an airline accounted for 90 per cent of peak flights for half
the period and 10 per cent for the other half, giving 50 per cent overall, a charge
based on the latter would be too low in the former sub-period and too high in the
latter sub-period.

Market power

Although increasing the concentration of slots at congested airports reduces the delay externality, this comes at a price: increasing concentration potentially increases market power. While the passenger might benefit from the optimisation of flight schedules that concentration allows for, this could be at the expense of fare increases unrelated to the underlying costs of the hub system. In the US, for example, although airlines compete across their respective hubs, so that many passengers have a choice of flights via competing hubs, such choice does not extend to those passengers starting or terminating their journeys at a hub airport. US studies have shown that such passengers appear to pay fare premiums, although it is arguable whether these premiums reflect scarcity rents and the extraction of consumer surplus by yield management (price discrimination) techniques.

Such is the sophistication of price discrimination using airline computer reservation systems (CRS) that some have argued that the outcome in a monopolistic market is a level of output (and thus a combined level of consumer and producer surplus) similar to that which would prevail in a competitive market (Button, 2002). Because airlines have the ability to discriminate between passengers with different preferences, the effect is to remove in large measure the distinction between the (declining) marginal revenue curves and the average revenue curves. In seeking to fill capacity, the airline will increase output until the marginal cost of providing for the additional passenger is equal to average revenue, which is the competitive outcome.

This suggests that a situation has evolved where concentration might have a benign impact on fares because airlines, even airlines with market power, act in an allocatively efficient manner when pricing their product.[13] Arguably, this might appear to make competition policy redundant in the airline sector, but it does of course ignore the issue of productive efficiency: although airlines (because of incentives to fill seats) might be producing at optimal levels of output given their respective cost bases, costs might nevertheless be at inefficient levels, a possibility borne out by many studies of airline costs.[14] This suggests that the real importance of competition in the airline industry is to bear down on cost inefficiencies. To the extent that this can be achieved through capital market disciplines or, as recent findings by Morrison (2001) suggest, without the need for head-to-head competition, a more relaxed view of slot concentration at congested airports can be taken.[15]

The US trading markets

A secondary market approach is used currently at a small number of busy airports in the US as an alternative to rationing by queue. Because the demand for runway use was particularly high at Kennedy (JFK) and La Guardia (LGA) in New York City, at O'Hare (ORD) in Chicago and at Washington Ronald Reagan National

---

13 Note, however, that the dominant airline can extract monopoly rents in different forms. For example, it could do so by imposing delay costs on passengers in order to realise cost savings in the use of equipment and staff. However, the extent to which the airline monopolist would wish to extract rents by increasing passenger delays is probably limited; such delays are correlated with operational delays that, in turn, increase airline costs. Clearly such increases are offset by strategic gains from scale and scope economies and from revenue enhancements that flow from adopting a hub system with a pronounced peak pattern of operations. Nevertheless, dominance provides the opportunity for inefficient behaviour.

14 See, for example, Ng and Seabright (2001) and Windle (1991).

15 This suggests that policies that encourage the establishment of low-cost airlines and the privatisation of state airlines have a major role to play in increasing the efficiency of the airline sector as a whole.

(DCA) many years ago the authorities stepped in to prescribe a limit on the number of flights at these airports during specified hours. The limit was known as the 'high density rule'. The rule did not itself provide a method for allocating the authorised number of runway operations between airlines, and a number of different approaches were tried without a great deal of success before trading markets were sanctioned at the end of 1985.

The market was restricted to slots used for *domestic* services which in turn were divided into two groups: air carrier slots and commuter carrier slots (originally operated by aircraft with 56 or fewer seats). Slots assigned for use by commuter carriers could not be purchased by air carriers. In addition, slots used for subsidised 'essential air services' were excluded from the market. The regulations stipulated that any person was entitled to purchase, sell or mortgage a slot, or to lease on a temporary basis, and third parties such as local communities could be included in the transactions.[16] However, slots not used for a stipulated minimum time in a two-month period had to be returned to the FAA; that is to say, carriers had to 'use or lose' their slot. Surrendered slots, or others becoming available, were assigned to a pool and reallocated using a lottery but with 25 per cent initially offered to new entrants.

These basic terms were introduced in April 1986 when airlines started to buy and sell those slots that they were holding as of 16 December 1985. Later, small amendments were made to the regulations. From January 1993 slots had to be used for 80 per cent of the time in a two-month period (it was previously 65 per cent) and the definition of those entitled to slots from the reserved pool was broadened to include incumbent carriers with few slots. In addi-

---

16   For further details, see Starkie (1992 and 1994).

tion, restrictions were introduced to prevent slots intended for new entrants being acquired by incumbents. Other amendments adjusted the distinction between air carrier and commuter slots, a distinction that was introduced originally in order to strike a balance between maximising the economic use of runway resources and preserving services to smaller communities. The aircraft size threshold for the use of commuter slots was increased, particularly at ORD.

During the 1990s, however, the US Department of Transportation was subject to constant pressure from politicians and lobbyists seeking privileged access for either small communities or for competing airlines. As a consequence, exemptions were granted at LGA; a new entrant, Jet Blue, obtained a significant number of slots at JFK; and there were some exemptions granted at ORD. In spite of, or perhaps because of these concessions, pressures continued, and eventually Congress passed ARI21 leading to a radical change in policy and proposals to phase out much of the high density rule. The rule was eliminated at ORD from July 2002. It is to be removed from JFK and LGA in 2007, although it will continue to remain in place at DCA. In the meantime, open entry has been declared for regional jets, except at DCA. This has led to a huge expansion of such flights and, in turn, to very serious delays, with the result that the FAA has intervened and imposed a lottery on a temporary basis at LGA. Not surprisingly, these changes in the regulations, and the phasing out of flight limits in 2002 at ORD, have resulted in much reduced activity in the slot markets. At LGA the value of slots has been diluted by the various exemptions and, more recently, by the lottery.

Table 2 **Summary of air carrier slot leases and sales at US high-density airports, 1986–92**

	Leases		Sales	Total transactions
	<6 months	>6 months		
1986	163	79	375	617
1987	617	5	152	774
1988	612	58	64	734
1989	1,259		290	1,549
1990	1,294		403	1,607
1991	1,468		477	1,945
1992	1,178		310	1,488

Source: Starkie (1992) and Wolf (1999: 126).

Analysis of the trading markets

Data on air carrier slot transactions for the period from 1986, when the regulation was first introduced, to 1992, prior to the amendment of the regulation, are shown in Table 2. During the first six to nine months, there was an initial surge of sales as air carriers acquired the slots they believed they could use best and disposed of those that could be sold profitably. This initial phase was followed by a decline in the number of outright sales while the number of leases grew, particularly short-term leases, possibly reflecting a requirement for the use of a slot at limited times of the year only. After 1988, however, sales once more increased such that in both 1990 and 1991 they exceeded the total for 1986. The number of lease transactions also increased considerably between 1988 and 1989, and thereafter stabilised at the higher level. Separate information is also available for the ring-fenced slots used by commuter carriers, but only for the first three years (Table 3). Commuter carriers appeared at that time to be more inclined to buy and sell, rather than to lease, and some new commuter

Table 3 **Summary of commuter carrier slot leases and sales at US high-density airports, 1986–8**

	< 6 months	> 6 months	Sales	Total transactions
1986	54	2	103	159
1987	3	0	20	23
1988	17	0	82	99

Source: Starkie (1992).

airlines took the opportunity to enter the market. A significant number of slots were held by non-carriers; some airlines mortgaged their slots to financial institutions while local communities also took the opportunity to purchase.

At a superficial level these, albeit limited, data appear to bear out the view of the US General Accounting Office (USGAO, 1996) that there had been few entrants into the four US airports and that established airlines have increased their share of slots. There do appear to have been relatively few outright sales, particularly when account is also taken of transfers as a result of mergers and other statistical quirks (see Starkie, 1992: 15). However, the evidence has to be balanced by other considerations. First, airlines when entering the market need more than just a runway slot; they also need access to gates, counter space and handling facilities. In contrast to the general situation in Europe, facilities such as gates are leased at US airports and spare capacity is not always available. Second, declining sales and lack of entry have to be interpreted in the context of developments in the airline market as a whole. Generally throughout the period the US airline industry was consolidating as a result of exits or mergers and acquisitions, and in these circumstances it might be argued that entry at the 'high density rule' airports was less likely to occur. Third, the emphasis on the short-term leasing of slots rather than on outright sales might be explained by the market approaching equilibrium; within the overall constraints of limited capacity, the most profitable opportunities were being exploited to a very large extent by the established airlines. Therefore, it is difficult to conclude from the general picture with limited data available that slots were used inefficiently and perhaps hoarded.

Kleit and Kobayashi (1996) have undertaken a more rigorous analysis of whether slots have been used efficiently by using data for Chicago O'Hare. Of the four US airports where slots are bought and sold, ORD has the most concentrated holding of slots (reflecting its role as an airline hub) and it is also the one airport where those airlines established before deregulation of the US domestic market have increased the number of slots held. The analysis, based on 1990 data, focused on the utilisation of slots. It specifically examined whether the two large dominant carriers (United and American) were using their slots more, or less, intensively than the smaller carriers: the usual market power argument would be that the dominant firm(s) have an incentive to restrict output which would be reflected in lower utilisation rates. Slot utilisation was measured in three ways: by the average rate at which slots were used; by whether leased slots were used more or less intensively than owned and operated slots; and by the average daily seat capacity per slot. The analysis indicated that the dominant carriers had a higher usage rate for their slots and that slots they leased out were used at an equal or higher rate than owned and operated slots. In other words, there was no indication that dominant carriers were hoarding poorly utilised slots, or were leasing slots to other airlines that would make less use of them. On the other hand, there was evidence that one of the two dominant carriers (United) was using, on average, smaller aircraft.[17] Therefore Kleit and Kobayashi were unable to confirm that their analysis unequivocally supported the argument that concentration had led to increased output from the slots concerned, but the conclusion they arrived at was that concentration in the slot market at ORD did not appear to be leading to anti-competitive behaviour. The evidence was considered more consistent with the hypothesis that it was efficiency considerations which were generating concentration.

Policy prescriptions

Established airlines operating at major airports appear to gain significant benefits from expanding their slot portfolios. Expansion is encouraged by the potential for economies of scale, scope and density from operating a network of services. Fixed costs are spread over more units of output and the characteristics of a connected network drive market demand, enhancing revenues. Passengers benefit from the reach of the network, from increased flight frequencies and from increasing opportunities for making on-line transfers.

Although the busier the airport the more likely it is to experience congestion, some of this delay can be self-imposed. By adding a flight, an airline potentially adds to the delay experienced by its other flights at that airport, but it takes this interaction into

---

17 This might be explained by differences in the markets served by dominant and non-dominant carriers. For example, holders of a smaller number of slots (e.g. Continental) might have used these for long-haul flights. Alternatively, the fleet used by United might not have been fully optimised in relation to the dynamics of the market because such adjustments are not always economic in the short term.

account when deciding upon the scale and timing of its schedules. The effect is to internalise the normal external costs associated with congestion. It follows that by increasing slot concentration, delay externalities are reduced. If airport charges were based on the marginal costs of use, including marginal costs of delay, a dominant airline adding to its slot portfolio at the expense of other airlines would capture in a reduction in airport charges the *positive* externality associated with its decision. In the absence of marginal cost pricing of runway use, the second-best solution would be to pay a Pigouvian subsidy to the slot-acquiring incumbent airline, equivalent to the reduction in the external costs of delay. In these circumstances it is to be questioned whether the common concerns of policy-makers that large incumbent airlines might use a secondary market to acquire more slots at the expense of small incumbents or new entrants are not misplaced.

There is a genuine dilemma here. Slot concentration is driven by efficiency considerations, and would appear to offer considerable gains. But, at capacity-constrained airports, if a secondary market achieves efficiencies through facilitating slot concentration, by the same token it also has the effect of reducing opportunities for service competition at the route level. Competition has then to come from alternative hub airports probably equally dominated by one or two airlines, or from secondary airports used by low-cost carriers. This competition can be less effective, especially for short-haul flights and for those passengers originating or terminating their landside journeys close to the hub airport.[18] On the other hand, the sophistication of CRS-driven yield manage-

---

18 Airport competition is a relatively neglected issue that warrants more attention, if only in the light of the arguments presented in this paper. See also Starkie (2002).

ment techniques does enable airlines to capture rents (consumer surplus) through extensive price discrimination, so that the normal adverse efficiency consequences of limited competition, the curtailment of output, might be much less in this particular case. The situation is complicated, however; airlines could exploit their dominance by surreptitiously imposing delays on passengers, the effect of which is a loss of efficiency. Although it is argued that delays at hub airports represent an efficient equilibrium between the benefits of concentrating flights into narrow windows of time and the marginal costs of increasing delay, this is not necessarily so if the passenger is poorly informed about expected delays and published schedules are too optimistic.[19] But in such a case the remedy does not lie in imposing constraints on the use of slots.

Where should the balance lie between the undoubted benefits of concentrating slot holdings and the potential for abuse of the dominance that concentration facilitates? The answer is difficult and to an extent circumstantial. At airports like Heathrow, or JFK, both with capacity fully utilised for much of the time, but with the largest airline(s) occupying only a modest share of the total number of slots, there would seem to be much to be gained by allowing slot concentration through the operation of a secondary market. The diminution of the congestion externality alone is a powerful argument for doing so, but there might also be large gains from improving the timing and the schedule coordination of the dominant airline(s). In these circumstances, to impede slot concentration by legal or administrative constraints is likely to lead to significant losses of efficiency. On the other hand, at

---

19 An airline could, for example, publish optimistic schedules (which influence passenger demand) and use the delay imposed on passengers to complete rotations on longer-haul routes, thereby obtaining better equipment utilisation.

a capacity-constrained airport heavily dominated by one airline group, such as at Amsterdam Schiphol, the balance is much finer; there are probably diminishing returns from further concentration, but increasing risks from a less competitive environment that are potentially harmful to consumers. In these circumstances, with the overwhelming majority of slots in the hands of one airline, it might not be appropriate to allow the dominant airline to purchase further slots in a secondary market without showing just cause.

Conclusions

The characteristics of airline networks are such that major airports frequently develop as major locations for the transfer of passengers between flights. They become hub airports, and because of capacity constraints they frequently experience congestion. At such a congested airport, the tendency will be for a single airline (or occasionally two airlines) to dominate. When transferring between flights passengers prefer to change between aircraft belonging to the same airline; on-line transfers are generally preferred to interlining; and, since the number of potential connections increases exponentially with the number of the markets served by the hub airline, the hub dominant airline has an incentive to expand its network. This characteristic, together with potential production economies associated with the scale of the network and the attractions of higher service frequencies, means that the hub network operated by a dominant airline has many of the characteristics of a natural monopoly.

The development of the natural monopoly network can be stymied, however, by the difficulties of gaining access to runway slots which, the US apart, are allocated primarily on the basis of so-called historic rights. This would not matter if charges for the use of airport infrastructure reflected the marginal cost of use, in which case the price mechanism would allocate slots to those who derive most value from their use. But airport charges are rarely based on marginal cost and there remains considerable opposition to such an approach. Consequently, the allocation of airport slots is frequently sub-optimal. It is a situation that can be rectified, however, by allowing airlines to trade slots in secondary markets. Such markets have been operating at four US airports since 1985 and the indications are that these markets have effected a more efficient distribution and use of slots. In essence, given the constraints on correct pricing signals for the use of scarce airport capacity, secondary markets for slots would appear to be an important way of satisfying the dynamics involved in airline markets and an important means for discovering the efficient scale of the network natural monopoly.

Nevertheless, a one-size-fits-all approach is not necessarily appropriate. Opportunities for the reallocation of slots allowed for by a formal trading market are likely to be of greatest value at those congested airports still used by a large number of airlines, and where no single airline has a majority holding of slots. At these airports, in addition to the realisation of network economies, consolidating slot ownership is likely to reduce significantly the external costs of delay. In contrast, when most slots at a major airport are in the hands of a single carrier, both the potential gains from trade and the positive externalities from slot concentration will be less, and the potential for abuse of a dominant position greater. In these latter circumstances, a trading market is much less likely, although by no means unlikely, to lead to more efficient outcomes.

References

Bailey, E, and D. Liu (1995), 'Airline Consolidation in Consumer Welfare', *Eastern Economic Journal*, fall: 463–76.

Borenstein, S. (1988), 'On the Efficiency of Competitive Markets for Operating Licences', *Quarterly Journal of Economics*, May: 357–85.

Brueckner, J. K. (2002), 'Internalisation of Airport Congestion', *Journal of Air Transport Management*, May: 141–7.

Button, K. J. (2002), 'Debunking Some Common Myths about Airport Hubs', *Journal of Air Transport Management*, May: 177–88.

CAA (2002), *Heathrow, Gatwick and Stansted Airports' Price Caps, 2003–2008: CAA recommendations to the Competition Commission*, London.

Economics-Plus Limited and GRA Inc. (2000), *An Economic Assessment of the IATA Interline System*, report, IATA, Geneva.

Hogan, O., K. Feighan and D. Starkie (2002), *Off-Peak Landing and Take-off Charges and Aircraft Classification*, report, Commission for Aviation Regulation, Dublin, February (at www.aviationreg.ie).

Kleit, A., and B. Kobayashi (1996), 'Market Failure or Market Efficiency? Evidence on Airport Slot Usage', in B. McMullen (ed.), *Research in Transportation Economics*, JAI Press, Connecticut.

Mayer, C., and T. Sinai (2002), *Network Effects, Congestion Externalities, and Air Traffic Delays: Or Why All Delays Are Not Evil*, NBER Working Paper Series, January.

McGowan, F., and P. Seabright (1989), 'Deregulating European Airlines', *Economic Policy*, October: 283–344.

Morrison, S. A. (2001), 'Actual, Adjacent, and Potential

Competition: Estimating the Full Effect of Southwest Airlines', *Journal of Transport Economics & Policy*, May: 239–56.

Morrison, S. A., and C. Winston (1986), *The Economic Effects of Airline Deregulation*, Brookings Institute, Washington, DC.

Ng, C. K., and P. Seabright (2001), 'Competition, Privatisation and Productive Efficiency: Evidence from the Airline Industry', *Economic Journal*, July: 591–619.

Starkie, D. (1992), *Slot Trading at United States Airports*, a report for the DG VII of the European Commission, City Publications, London.

Starkie, D. (1994), 'Developments in Transport Policy: the US Market in Airport Slots', *Journal of Transport Economics & Policy*, September: 325–9.

Starkie, D. (2002), 'Airport Regulation and Competition', *Journal of Air Transport Management*, January: 63–72.

Starkie, D., and D. Thompson (1985), 'The Airports' Policy White Paper: Privatisation & Regulation', *Fiscal Studies*: 30–42.

Turvey, R. (2000), 'Infrastructure Access Pricing and Lumpy Investments', *Utilities Policy*: 207–18.

United States General Accounting Office (USGAO) (1996), *Airline Deregulation: Barriers to Entry Continue to Limit Competition in Several Key Domestic Markets*, report to US Senate.

Windle, R. J. (1991), 'The World's Airlines: A Cost and Productivity Comparison', *Journal of Transport Economics & Policy*, January: 31–49.

Wolf, H. (1999), 'Tackling Congestion and Environmental Problems', in W. Pfhaler et al. (eds), *Airports and Air Traffic Regulation, Privatisation and Competition*, Peter Lang, Frankfurt.

3 THE ROLE OF MARKET FORCES IN THE ALLOCATION OF AIRPORT SLOTS
Tom Bass

Introduction

The purpose of this paper is to examine the extent to which greater use could be made of market forces in the allocation of scarce runway capacity at airports. It suggests that, while there are major practical limitations to radical market solutions, the role of the market should be reinforced. There is a particular need for a freer market at those airports that have a shortage of capacity but are not yet 'super-congested'. Finally, the paper discusses what might happen to the proceeds of a price-based system and considers the implications for airport operators of alternative approaches.

The current situation

The existing system of slot allocation has its origins in the arrangements that IATA made, originally to facilitate interlining, but which were subsequently used to manage congestion. The basis of these arrangements was what became known as grandfather rights, under which an airline that held and used a slot in the previous year was entitled to use it – or exchange it for another one – in the next year.

As congestion built up and as airline markets were liberalised, the European Commission became increasingly concerned that this process was anti-competitive. In response IATA modified its Scheduling Procedures Guide to require some unused slots to go to new entrants. However, the Commission decided that it needed to take its own action and produced a code of conduct governing the process of slot allocation at all airports within the EU. This was swiftly followed by a formal regulation – EC Council Regulation No. 95/93.

In the negotiations that led up to the regulation, Member States were anxious to preserve the continuity and practical efficiency of the IATA system and were unwilling to dilute grandfather rights. As a result the regulation built on the IATA principles, including grandfather rights: indeed, Virgin and others have argued that by adopting grandfather rights the Commission gave them added force.

The regulation sought to encourage new entry in two main ways. First it discouraged slot hoarding by imposing stricter 'use it or lose it' conditions under which an airline that failed to use a slot on at least 80 per cent of occasions would lose it. Second, it required new, returned or unused slots to be put into a pool, and half of these to be made available to new entrants. However, a new entrant was very narrowly defined, the number of slots to which each was entitled was very limited, and the pool consisted largely of slots that were not already used and were therefore mainly at less attractive times. Thus its effect on new entry was only token.

The whole issue soon became topical again because the regulation itself required the Commission to review it. It was also generally recognised that, if enabling new entry was one of the purposes of the regulation, the new arrangements did not suffice.

In January 2001 the Commission published a proposal to revise the regulation. The proposal made a distinction between practical issues that could be addressed straight away and the need for a more radical review of slot allocation.

The proposal put forward changes designed to clarify the regulation and enforce it more effectively. It emphasised that the use of slots did not constitute property rights; slots were simply entitlements to access at specific times. It also put forward some detailed changes, for example on the definition of new entrants and on issues such as noise and regional services. All these proposals were in the context of the current philosophy, based primarily on grandfather rights and on the premise that slots may be exchanged but not unilaterally transferred or sold.

In parallel with the proposal the Commission announced that it would reconsider the fundamental basis of the regulation. In April 2002 it called for tenders for a study to assess the effects of different slot allocation systems, and the appointed consultants have now begun work.

These initiatives by the Commission have kept the debate moving. While a majority of Member States appear to be against radical change, the UK in particular has considered the possibility of secondary trading and slot auctions. The Department of the Environment, Transport and the Regions (DETR) has engaged consultants, and the CAA advocated market-based solutions in its paper 'The Implementation of Secondary Slot Trading', published in November 2001.

At the heart of the debate is the obvious fact that any system for allocating scarce capacity will create gainers and losers.

The gainers in the current system

The beneficiaries of the system are clearly those airlines that have large slot holdings at busy airports. They hold assets that have a big – sometimes huge – and appreciating market value. Provided they actually use the slots that they are entitled to keep or exchange them – whether or not they can be deemed to have legal ownership.

The incumbents' freedom to use their slots as they wish means that they face internal questions as to how to make best use of them. They will naturally use them on higher- rather than lower-yielding routes, with a consequent bias towards longer routes, international services, larger aircraft, business passengers, etc. The example of Heathrow shows this most clearly. BA progressively shifted lower-yielding flights – including some long-haul flights – and services that faced weaker competition to Gatwick, and pulled out of the Republic of Ireland altogether. Likewise British Midland dropped many of its less well-used domestic routes and built up its international services, while Virgin concentrated its high-yield services at Heathrow and operated the others from Gatwick. New shifts happen with each new timetable.

The slot regulation allows slot exchanges but does not allow sales or what it terms 'unilateral transfers' – i.e. direct transfers to another airline without any slots being transferred in return. However, everyone accepts that these occur, sometimes for very large – but inevitably undisclosed – sums. Again this favours incumbents since the seller reaps the proceeds while the buyer is in a market that is closed to new entrants.

The losers in the current system

All this gives rise to three main categories of losers.

- Users of thin, generally regional, services which the airlines displace to make room for more profitable routes.
- New entrants, who cannot get into the airport on the scale they need or in some cases at all.
- Users of routes where more head-to-head competition would stimulate new or better products or lower fares.

A fourth possible category of loser is an airline such as EasyJet, which has no plans to use the congested airports in question but which sees the lack of a legitimate market in slots as maintaining low-fare competition on short-haul routes on a scale that would not exist in the face of market forces. This proposition has recently been given more force by the increasing availability of low and quite flexible fares at Heathrow.

The present role of market forces

The fact that slot allocation is subject to such detailed restrictions and guidelines does not mean that market forces are not already operating. By allowing airlines to manage and exchange slots the regulation creates an internal market within airlines, and also a more limited market between incumbent airlines. Moreover, the impracticability of enforcing the prohibition on slot sales means that the market is more active than the regulation originally intended. Thus the present dilemma is not about whether market forces should work at all but about whether they should be limited and whether they would deliver all that is expected of them.

It is natural to ask why an open market should not be used for slots just as it is for any other scarce commodity. The accepted basis of Western economies is that open markets both give holders of scarce resources a powerful incentive to use them efficiently or to forgo them and enable new entrants to bid for them. The threat of new entry is probably the most powerful mechanism for stimulating efficiency and responsiveness to the consumer, particularly in an industry that is prone to oligopoly. Except where there are social arguments to the contrary, as for example in health, education, welfare or regional development, or where there are concerns about the competitive structure of the market, the price mechanism is normally preferred to administrative rationing where it is a practical proposition. What is different about airport slots?

Limits to what market forces can achieve

One of the concerns about the present system is that, because incumbent airlines manage their slots to their own advantage, the first routes that they drop in favour of more profitable opportunities tend to be politically sensitive regional services. Although these may be replaced by flights to another airport serving the same big city, there will be some loss of amenity and such replacements will not always be commercially viable.

However, the reason that these services are vulnerable is that existing market forces are working against them. Intensification of these forces could only add to the pressure. The slot regulation allows for the 'ring-fencing' of some regional services: the French government has used this but the UK government has made it consistently clear that it will not. Regional services will continue to be squeezed out of congested airports unless they are heavily subsidised or receive direct government protection.

There may also be competition concerns. One of the main premises of advocates of a freer market is that new entry will take place because incumbents will have to consider the real value of their holdings and will not be able, or may not wish, to bid for slots on their present scale. This will almost certainly be true in some cases. We know from the experience of present market pressures at Heathrow that some of the weaker or smaller airlines, and those without a significant strategic presence there, have sold slots for very large sums. Against this it is difficult to see how and why their stronger counterparts would hold back. The little evidence we have in real life comes from the limited experience of sales and auctions in the US where, after preliminary skirmishing, the dominant airlines became the main buyers and increased their slot shares.

The possibility that more open markets will add to rather than reduce concentration at airports with strong home carriers is one of the main issues facing the Commission in its review. Virgin, one of the main critics of grandfather rights, has suggested that even a gradual approach to market-based solutions may require parallel measures to moderate or reduce the share of dominant carriers. In some cases to allow an efficient dominant carrier to further increase its market share at the expense of weaker competitors may be the efficient solution. On the other hand it certainly reduces the stimulus of competition and creates greater opportunity for the abuse of a dominant position: some argue that the increase in the share of a dominant firm is itself prima facie evidence of such abuse.

The continuing disagreement on this issue is encapsulated by recent advice to the DETR. The CAA, guided by a fundamental faith in the inherent efficiency of free markets, believes that competition issues are for the competition authorities and that these should act only on a case-by-case basis. By contrast, consultants

DotEcon, while favouring market mechanisms, have advised the DETR that they 'should not be introduced without measures to prevent excessive concentration of slot holdings'.

In principle such wide issues of airline competition policy should obviously be considered in the round and not treated ad hoc as an adjunct to the narrower issue of slot allocation. However, EU Member States have widely differing views. Many of them put less weight than does the UK on competition issues, and some would oppose any change that they would expect to undermine what they regard as their airlines at their hubs. Against this background it is unlikely that the Commission could deliver a new package that involved enforced reductions of existing shares, whether or not it thought it the right thing to do.

On a more positive note, the history of airline deregulation in Europe shows that, if well handled, consensus can be found for step change and the measured introduction of market forces.

The debate on the new regulation has also brought out a new concept of super-congestion. This draws a distinction between those airports which are not yet full and where encouraging market forces could play an important part in moving out sufficient existing or future marginal users to create additional capacity, and those like Heathrow, where any scheme would be unlikely to bring demand and supply into equilibrium. Indeed, the market-clearing price at Heathrow would have to be extremely high, involving large multiples of the present regulated charges. It is also significant that some of the bigger, but not super-congested, airports have relatively weak base carriers that would be under pressure to improve or retrench.

Finally, there is a whole series of practical problems about explicit use of the price mechanism, and these have been exhaustively analysed elsewhere. Their general flavour is described below, but two main points need to be made. First, the practical difficulties tend to be much more daunting for the more root-and-branch solutions than for the evolutionary ones. Second, the priority should be to consider what the various approaches could be expected to achieve and deal in detail with the practicalities afterwards. That said, an important contribution could be achieved by relatively uncomplicated measures, particularly at the less congested airports.

- International constraints: much of the analysis of price has been undertaken by economists to whom treating scarcity value as a cost is second nature. However academically respectable pricing for scarcity may be, it implies large rewards for the owners of the scarce product and it is unlikely that those who pay the charges will interpret the requirements in international treaties and conventions that refer to 'reasonable' charges in that way.
- Slot combinations: airlines need slots in combinations to be able to mount routes or networks, particularly non-residents, who will have portfolios too small to be managed across a system. Whether sold by posted price or by auction, slots will have to be offered in workable combinations. These will also have to accommodate, as the present system does, other capacity constraints on stands and terminals, or there will need to be a parallel process to deal with them.
- Stability: airlines, governments and other interests have been concerned that radical approaches, e.g. simultaneous sale of most or all of the slots, would create total uncertainty about which airlines and networks would emerge. Governments will insist on moving gradually, if at all.

- Multiple sales: if auctions are used airlines will at first have little guidance on how much to bid. Similarly, with posted prices the airport or government would not know what to charge to avoid the twin problems of multiple offers or unsold slots. Thus the process would be wrong first time and would have to be iterative.

Some of these problems could be alleviated by intermediate or gradual solutions. For example, a posted pricing scheme could be run alongside the present administered scheme, or something like it. Similarly, the initial auctions could be for small proportions of the total slots, although someone would have to decide which specific slots were to go on the market.

The way forward

The discussion so far has sought to show that, while total reliance on free market forces is no panacea and would in some cases lead to unintended and possibly anti-competitive effects, the present arrangements are evidently anti-competitive. If interpreted literally, and fortunately they are not, they would prevent significant new entry and put little pressure on inefficient airlines, or airlines using their slots inefficiently, to release them. However, even applied in the present pragmatic manner, they still blunt these efficiency incentives, and the Commission's objective should be to introduce practical reforms that will increase the role of the market. It is unlikely that the most radical of the suggested reforms would stand any chance of political acceptance: in particular even those governments with strong competition credentials will resist any forced reduction of slot holdings on what they still regard as their national airlines. Even if they were accepted some of the results would be contrary to the original objectives of change. Of still greater importance is the fact that practical problems of organisation and negotiation would limit the pace of change in any event.

This does not mean that it is impossible to make significant improvements. The extent to which market forces have already found a path through the administered systems suggests that there are ways of harnessing them that are deliverable and which would be beneficial, particularly at airports that are not super-congested.

The present slot regulation prohibits, but is unable to prevent, open trading for money between incumbents and makes it difficult, but not impossible, between incumbents and new entrants. Both these constraints should be removed. This would not solve the problem of excess demand at the super-congested airports, but it would encourage further turnover to the extent that it has not already happened covertly. At some other airports there is a serious need to give weaker or marginal users the spur and the opportunity to make way for more effective replacements.

This is the simplest and most immediately beneficial reform that the Commission could adopt. It is necessary in any case to deal with the anomaly that sales have to be dressed up as exchanges. Open sale would also bring additional benefits since it would make it more likely that an open-market price would be revealed, thus making any subsequent moves to a more thorough-going price mechanism easier, and it would also enable a closer eye to be kept on the competition implications.

If the international problems could be overcome, open trading could be reinforced by posted prices. These could initially be set quite low, and certainly far too low to clear the market, but they would be high enough to take some of the airlines, or some of their bids, out of the queue. Again, such a trial would not only contribute to efficient use but would ease the transition to more radical solutions if these became feasible.

It is unrealistic to suggest auctions at this stage, despite their obvious theoretical attractions. This is because there is little prospect of their being acceptable to the governments that have in the end to agree the changes and because the practical problems, even with a partial auction, are formidable. They should certainly not be introduced without serious attention to the competitive effects, and this of itself is a barrier to their introduction in the foreseeable future.

Proceeds of sale

If open sales of slots are introduced one of the obvious questions is who should get the proceeds. To those whose prime concern is economic efficiency this is a secondary problem, but it is important nonetheless.

The present system suppresses the issue since the actual beneficiaries of the shortage of slots are the airlines, but the actual value is hidden in intra- and inter-company trading. On an open market the natural recipient is the provider of the capacity – the airport – but why should airport shareholders make a windfall profit from scarce supply? The airports cannot reasonably expect to reap this reward, particularly where they are subject to price regulation specifically to prevent abuse of their dominant position.

One suggestion is that the proceeds should go to airports, but that they should be required to commit them to reliever projects elsewhere. The history of airport development should warn us against 'Fields of Dreams' developments – massively premature, ambitious or misdirected projects that rely on supply creating its own demand. This idea also carries the presumption that the owner of the constrained airport should be the developer or, alternatively, that the government should do it itself or fund a third party to do so.

The most likely eventual solution is that the government would take the proceeds on the basis that, if no one else has a tenable claim, the taxpayer is the worthiest recipient. The irony is that it is the government which is usually the arbiter of whether new runways should receive planning permission. These windfall gains could only add to the already powerful incentives to refuse permission.

Implications for airports

Airports are in an odd position with respect to slot allocation. They partly determine the number of slots available, since the physical layout of the airport and the availability of rapid turn-offs, etc., are crucial factors. So too is the ability of the terminals, stands and other facilities to accept the traffic that the runway accommodates. However, once the capacity has been determined, it is often the airlines which decide how capacity is allocated since they often administer the EU slot regulation. In many respects this suits the airports, which would not wish to be drawn into arguments between their customers or, in extreme cases, between governments. They also know that they would not be allowed to keep the proceeds of the sale of the scarce capacity. Nevertheless, airports do have a direct financial interest. They will generally aim to maximise their revenues, and this means maximising the use made of commercial facilities that are not directly regulated, including shops, VIP lounges, etc., as well as maximising the overall number of passengers. By and large the airlines have the same interest, although some of their prime passengers, such as domestic business travellers, may contribute less to commercial revenue than long-haul leisure passengers.

However, it is quite clear that airports will benefit if freer market forces enable the less efficient and less market-responsive airlines to be replaced by more vigorous competitors. There will be further benefits to airports in those countries where the legacy of history means that resident airlines do not pay full charges. Thus the interests of airports as well as of users will almost certainly be better served by a further shift towards market forces.

4 SLOT ALLOCATION: A RADICAL SOLUTION
Barry Humphreys

Introduction

The rules governing the allocation of slots at airports within the EU are covered by EC Council Regulation no. 95/93 that came into force in January 1993. One of the objectives of the regulation is to increase competition in the aviation market by enabling new-entrant carriers to serve their chosen destinations. The text provides for a revision of the regulation by July 1997. Despite manifest problems with the application of the regulation, which were identified in a report prepared for the European Commission by Coopers and Lybrand as long ago as 1995, we are still some way from a revised regulation. Yet more consultants are currently at work for the Commission.

A failure to tackle the issue of slots, particularly at highly congested airports such as London's Heathrow, risks consumers losing the full benefits of liberalisation. This essay examines why slot reform is so important, identifies the scale and nature of the problem, considers some of the options for reform often canvassed, and makes proposals for a more radical solution to the problem.

The importance of slot reform

At the heart of the problem of slot allocation is the dominant position of individual so-called 'flag carriers' in their national markets. Air France is dominant in France, Lufthansa in Germany, BA in the UK, etc. Such dominance has not arisen because these airlines provide a better or cheaper service than their smaller competitors. It is largely the result of the considerable government support that these airlines have received over the years, resulting in extensive route networks and control over distribution systems that other airlines are unable to match. Nowhere is this more evident than in the case of airport slots. These dominant airlines have enjoyed free use of valuable rights to which would-be competitors have no, or only limited, access. This has enabled flag carriers to establish a virtual stranglehold on the market to the detriment of smaller competitors and the travelling public. It has cemented in place a market structure that is failing to provide the degree of real competition required.

Nature of the problem

The long-term solution to the problem is to bring demand and supply for slots into balance, by creating more capacity. Environmental concerns mean that this is unlikely to offer an easy or timely resolution, as the current debate on the need for additional airport capacity in the UK illustrates all too well. Even with no major impediment, which the Terminal 5 saga showed to be an optimistic assumption, and the political will to press ahead, a third short runway at Heathrow is unlikely to be available much before 2012. The immediate focus therefore should be on making better and more efficient use of the existing capacity.

Most of the major airports in Europe have managed to increase declared hourly capacities in recent years (see Table 4). In many

Table 4 **Declared hourly runway capacities for summer busy periods**

Airport	1993	1995	1998
Single runways			
Gatwick	36–45	40–47	42–48
Geneva	30	30	35
Dusseldorf	30	30	34
Milan (Linate)	24	22	32
Athens	30	30	30
Parallel runways			
Heathrow	77–79	77–81	75–84
Paris (CDG)	76	76	76–84
Copenhagen	74	76	81
Munich	68	70	80
Frankfurt	68	70	76
Paris (Orly)	70	70	70
Brussels	53	60	64
Rome	50	56	63
Milan (Malpensa)	30	30	26
Converging runways			
Stockholm	63	66	70
Zurich	60	60	66
Vienna	30	45	54
Madrid	35	30–50	50
Barcelona	28	30	47
Hamburg	40	42	45

Source: CAA, CAP 685, 1998, based on IATA data.

cases, however, such increases are modest compared with demand. Runway capacity is fully, or nearly fully, subscribed over most of the operating day at Barcelona, Brussels, Düsseldorf, Frankfurt, London (Heathrow and Gatwick), Madrid and Zurich. At other airports listed in Table 4, runway capacity is scarce for at least one hour during the busy periods. As environmental pressures increase, and the demand for air transport grows, airport infrastructure constraints are likely to become even more of a problem.

The problems are particularly acute at London's Heathrow

Table 5 **New-entrant airlines at Heathrow, 1995–9**

	Airline	Services per week
1995	Eva Airways	2
	Tajikistan Airways*	2
	DHL	1 (cargo)
	Alliance Airlines	2
	Akdeniz Airlines*	3 (off-peak charter)
	Turkmenistan Airlines	1
	Kazakhstan*	1
1996	Air Jamaica	3
	Air Baltic	1
	Polar Air	1 (cargo)
	Philippine Airlines	7
1997	Avianca	2 (late-night departures)
	Cronus Airlines	5
	Qatar Airlines	7 (late-night departures)
	DHL	1 (cargo)
1998	Georgian Airlines*	3 (late-night departures)
1999	Base Airlines	11 (BA franchise)
	Arkia	1
	Libyan Arab Airlines	1

*No longer operating

and Gatwick Airports. At Heathrow, for example, the CAA noted in its February 1995 report on slot allocation in the EU (CAP 644) that at peak times demand for slots exceeded supply by more than 30 per cent. The mismatch has grown significantly since then. The impact of the events of 11 September 2001, and BA's decision to downsize its Gatwick hub, may have reduced the extent of the problem at Gatwick, but this is a short-term phenomenon and unlikely to continue in the long term.

The effect on competition should not be underestimated. BA controls 38 per cent of the total slots at Heathrow, and possibly more following recent slot purchases reported in the press. While this represents a smaller proportion than many other European dominant carriers enjoy at their primary hubs, the UK's largest airline still has an extremely strong position at Heathrow. The situation during certain peak hours is even more marked.

Congestion at Heathrow represents a significant barrier to entry, making it difficult to challenge BA's dominant position. Heathrow is by far the most congested airport in Europe. Following changes to the Traffic Distribution Rules in 1991, several airlines (including Virgin Atlantic) successfully transferred services from Gatwick to Heathrow. This was, however, a one-off and only added to the congestion at Heathrow. Access to Heathrow has become increasingly difficult. A list of the new entrants at Heathrow in more recent years (see Table 5) shows clearly the very real problems that exist. The new services are overwhelmingly operated during off-peak periods, often at low frequencies and seat factors by weak competitors. By any measure they do not represent a significant improvement in the competitive environment.

It is true that several new-entrant carriers are using secondary airports such as Luton and Stansted, and most are apparently doing well. Realistically, however, this is very much a second-best option. Passengers, especially time-sensitive business passengers, clearly have a preference primarily for Heathrow, followed by Gatwick. Operating from secondary airports leaves BA's dominance virtually untouched, with the risk that it is able to exploit its dominant position to attack new entrants. The latter are unable to respond by attacking BA's base market.

The priority that the EU slot regulation gives to new entrants, tightly defined, fails to take sufficiently into account the overall competitive impact of those services for which new slots are made available. Smaller carriers like Virgin Atlantic do not qualify as new entrants, but have greater potential to challenge the dominant airline and provide more effective competition. These airlines have been held back by the shortage of slots. Virgin, for example, has about 2 per cent of Heathrow and Gatwick slots. It has been very difficult to add significantly to these slot holdings in recent years, with the result that some new services have had to be postponed.

This puts smaller airlines at a considerable competitive disadvantage to a dominant carrier like BA. BA can manipulate its large slot holding to maximise the competitive impact. It has, for example, transferred certain monopoly domestic services to Gatwick in order to increase frequencies on Heathrow transatlantic routes, where it faces more intense competition. This is not an option available to other airlines. Similarly, BA can take apparently almost worthless slots and, by combining them with other slots in its large portfolio, produce valuable opportunities. Again, this is not something other airlines at Heathrow can do.

Minimalist reform options

Two key features of the existing slot regulation are the principle of grandfather rights and the positive discrimination in favour of new entrants.

Grandfather rights allow an incumbent airline to keep its slots in perpetuity. Provided a slot is used on at least 80 per cent of occasions during the season, it can be retained for the next corresponding season. (Even if an airline does not use a slot 80 per cent of the time, it may still be possible to retain the slot.) Once a carrier has a slot there are very few limitations on the use to which it can be put. Where slots are newly created, or remain unused, they are placed in a slot pool; 50 per cent of these slots are reserved for new entrants.

There are two modest options for reform that are often canvassed. First, grandfather rights for newly created or unused slots returned to the pool could be abolished and those slots allocated either by means of the current system or by a system of primary trading. A more market-oriented approach certainly has attractions. Slots would go to those airlines that are likely to value them most. However, this option would do little more than tinker with the underlying problem since the overwhelming bulk of slots would remain with the incumbent carriers.

Each year more slots are produced as air traffic control and airport management efficiency improve, although some would argue that such growth may now be coming to an end failing radical change, such as the introduction of mixed-mode operations at Heathrow. In any case, these new slots come nowhere near to satisfying demand and are certainly insufficient to threaten BA's dominant position. Moreover, slots that are returned unused to the pool almost invariably tend to be the least commercially valuable. Finally, removing grandfather rights only from those slots that are more likely to be obtained by smaller airlines, while retaining them for the slots held by the dominant players, hardly seems fair to smaller airlines and is unlikely to do much to enhance competition.

The second modest reform often advocated is to extend secondary trading. Again this has attractions, in the sense that slots should go to those who value them most highly. However, it would do little to address the fundamental problem of an illiquid market, characterised by inadequate supply. If secondary trading were the answer to the industry's problems, those problems would long ago have largely disappeared. Airlines already engage in such trading, albeit usually hidden from view. Despite the highly publicised disagreement between the former EU Commissioners for Transport and Competition on the legality and acceptability of secondary trading, UK courts have now found it to be legal under the EU Slot Regulation.

As the former Competition Commissioner, Karel van Miert, has pointed out, a market requires sellers as well as buyers: 'In congested airports like Heathrow we know the buyers, but who are the sellers? The likelihood is that slots would be sold and bought only once, for the benefit of a few already dominant carriers.' US experience has similarly shown that slot trading can produce greater dominance by a small number of airlines. Use of the price mechanism to allocate these scarce resources could, therefore, have a perverse outcome unless accompanied by action on the supply side. Unconstrained use of the price mechanism in an illiquid market will favour dominant airlines with easier access to capital. Where other carriers are willing or forced to sell, the dominant airlines will always be able to outbid smaller carriers in the knowledge that the commercial risks are lower than they might otherwise be.

The main benefit from making the system of secondary trading more formal would be an improvement in transparency. However, even a reform that combined more transparent secondary trading with the abolition of grandfather rights for newly created slots, which at one stage appeared to be gaining favour in some quarters, would represent only a very modest step forward.

The radical reform option

If air services from congested airports are to be opened up to increased competition, then governments and regulators will need to address fundamentally the issue of grandfather rights. Virgin Atlantic has long lobbied for just such an approach.

As a contribution to the debate promoted by Readings 56, the main elements of Virgin's proposals for radical reform of the existing system of slot allocation are summarised below:

- In future grandfather rights should be limited to a fixed period of time, say ten or fifteen years.
- A certain proportion of all the slots at congested airports should be returned to the slot pool each year. These could either be randomly chosen or each airline might be required to return a similar proportion of its holding above a threshold (this would be necessary to ensure that the effect on smaller airlines was not disproportionate). For the purposes of illustration, if 10 per cent of the slots at an airport are returned each year, then after ten years all the slots would have been recirculated.
- All airlines would be free to bid for slots returned to the pool. Allocation would take place as at present at twice-yearly slot conferences held to determine schedules for the following summer or winter seasons. This process would continue to be run by an independent slot coordinator. There are issues about ensuring the availability of other corresponding airport facilities, but these should not be insurmountable.
- The existing slot conference arrangements would be used to enable airlines to match slots and to construct viable service patterns for the forthcoming season.
- The slot coordinator would require clear guidelines in order to allocate the pool slots. One option would be to use the current system, amended to remove the new-entrant anomaly

referred to above. There is no obvious reason why this would not work, although certainly the coordinator's job would become more difficult and complex. On the other hand, economic logic would seem to point inevitably to the sale of slots. The proceeds could go to the Exchequer, as is the case now in the bidding for radio, TV and mobile telephone franchises, or to the airport owner provided the regulator ensured that the windfall gain was passed on in full to the airport's customers, i.e. the airlines. This is preferable to the proceeds being received by the airlines giving up the slots. This would merely distort the market further in favour of the dominant carriers. Certainly, if an incumbent was able to bid for a slot for which it would otherwise receive payment, what it was prepared to pay would be artificially influenced.

On balance, Virgin Atlantic supports the sale of slots as the most appropriate method of allocation. This could raise about £700 million at Heathrow, even on relatively conservative assumptions. However, appropriation by the Exchequer in isolation would represent an additional tax on the travelling public, with no obvious benefit to the industry or consumers, and would be highly unpopular unless it was used to replace other taxes such as the Air Passenger Duty or redirected towards the industry in the form of additional infrastructure construction, support for increased public transport access to airports or payments to those adversely affected by air transport's growth.

The whole system would need to be subject to close scrutiny by the competition authorities to prevent anti-competitive or predatory behaviour, particularly by dominant airlines. The transparency of the system – and the ability to monitor and compare the

prices bid for particular slots – is critical to providing the necessary safeguards. There is an argument that a dominant airline at
an airport should not be allowed to increase its dominance by slot
purchase.

The advantages of a proposal along these lines are obvious.
Restricting grandfather rights would address directly the problem of supply and the current illiquidity of the market. There are,
however, vested interests that will favour the status quo, or some
strictly limited departure from it – namely those who already control large numbers of slots at Europe's most congested airports.
It is worth considering the arguments that are often deployed by
such opponents of reform.

First, *limited grandfather rights would amount to confiscation
without compensation of valuable assets.* Ownership of slots is a matter of dispute. The present UK Labour government has followed its
Conservative predecessor in maintaining that slots are not owned
by the airlines that use them. Certainly, until very recently, no
European airline included the value of its slots as assets in its annual accounts. (BA now includes in its accounts a value of £42 million for slots acquired for cash, but allocates no value to the bulk
of its slots acquired for nothing.) Moreover, if a carrier did own a
slot, it would not be logical for that slot to be confiscated should
the airline fail to use it intensively, as happens under the existing
EU Slot Regulation.

Second, it is maintained that *incumbents have invested significantly in the routes for which the slots are used and are thus responsible
for creating the value attached to them.* Flag carriers have more than
recovered the cost of their investment in developing routes. It is a
widely accepted rule of thumb within the industry that a new route
loses money in its first year, breaks even in the second and is mar-

ginally profitable in the third. Granting airlines rights to a slot for a fixed period of ten or fifteen years would ensure that the initial investment had long since been fully amortised. In any case, most of the equipment can be employed elsewhere or leased to other airlines. There is little fixed investment. In the final analysis, if a route has not made a healthy return on the initial investment after ten years, it should probably not have been operated in the first place, or should have been operated by a more efficient airline.

Third, *removing grandfather rights will disrupt service schedules and route networks and create uncertainty for passengers.* The proposal here avoids the problem as it is proposed that the changes should be phased in over a period of time. In any case, the risk of any inconvenience to passengers is small. If there is sufficient demand for a route to be served by an incumbent airline, then it should also be attractive to a new operator who might acquire the slots. It is worth noting that under the existing system, established dominant players have been prepared to switch services from one airport to another, and replace some short-haul routes with long-haul operations, in order to increase profitability. The reality is that if competition is to be encouraged and the market allowed to operate more freely, an element of instability is inevitable. Consumers may well consider that this is a price worth paying for better service and lower prices.

Conclusion

The European air transport industry has come a long way in recent years in breaking out of the regulatory straitjacket that inhibited its development for so long. Competition is increasing. Competitors continue to emerge who are able and willing to compete with the dominant flag carriers, to introduce innovative services and lower prices to the benefit of the travelling public. There is still, however, a long way to go, while the imperfections in this market remain. Governments and the regulatory authorities can play an important role in nurturing competition. In many European markets, and particularly on the denser routes that almost invariably involve at least one congested airport, competition could be increased dramatically and at a stroke by restricting grandfather rights to airport slots.

The willingness of governments to take action in this area is a test of their commitment to increase competition in air transport. It is true that many EU Member States will continue to back the interests of the incumbent flag carriers rather than support a more pro-competition solution. That is no reason for the UK, and the European Commission, not to advocate radical reform.

ABOUT THE IEA

The Institute is a research and educational charity (No. CC 235 351), limited by guarantee. Its mission is to improve understanding of the fundamental institutions of a free society with particular reference to the role of markets in solving economic and social problems.

The IEA achieves its mission by:

- a high-quality publishing programme
- conferences, seminars, lectures and other events
- outreach to school and college students
- brokering media introductions and appearances

The IEA, which was established in 1955 by the late Sir Antony Fisher, is an educational charity, not a political organisation. It is independent of any political party or group and does not carry on activities intended to affect support for any political party or candidate in any election or referendum, or at any other time. It is financed by sales of publications, conference fees and voluntary donations.

In addition to its main series of publications the IEA also publishes a quarterly journal, *Economic Affairs*, and has two specialist programmes – Environment and Technology, and Education.

The IEA is aided in its work by a distinguished international Academic Advisory Council and an eminent panel of Honorary Fellows. Together with other academics, they review prospective IEA publications, their comments being passed on anonymously to authors. All IEA papers are therefore subject to the same rigorous independent refereeing process as used by leading academic journals.

IEA publications enjoy widespread classroom use and course adoptions in schools and universities. They are also sold throughout the world and often translated/reprinted.

Since 1974 the IEA has helped to create a world-wide network of 100 similar institutions in over 70 countries. They are all independent but share the IEA's mission.

Views expressed in the IEA's publications are those of the authors, not those of the Institute (which has no corporate view), its Managing Trustees, Academic Advisory Council members or senior staff.

Members of the Institute's Academic Advisory Council, Honorary Fellows, Trustees and Staff are listed on the following page.

The Institute gratefully acknowledges financial support for its publications programme and other work from a generous benefaction by the late Alec and Beryl Warren.

The Institute of Economic Affairs
2 Lord North Street, Westminster, London SW1P 3LB
Tel: 020 7799 8900
Fax: 020 7799 2137
Email: iea@iea.org.uk
Internet: iea.org.uk

Other papers recently published by the IEA include:

WHO, What and Why?

Transnational Government, Legitimacy and the World Health Organization
Roger Scruton
Occasional Paper 113; ISBN 0 255 36487 3
£8.00

The World Turned Rightside Up

A New Trading Agenda for the Age of Globalisation
John C. Hulsman
Occasional Paper 114; ISBN 0 255 36495 4
£8.00

The Representation of Business in English Literature

Introduced and edited by Arthur Pollard
Readings 53; ISBN 0 255 36491 1
£12.00

Anti-Liberalism 2000

The Rise of New Millennium Collectivism
David Henderson
Occasional Paper 115; ISBN 0 255 36497 0
£7.50

Capitalism, Morality and Markets
Brian Griffiths, Robert A. Sirico, Norman Barry & Frank Field
Readings 54; ISBN 0 255 36496 2
£7.50

A Conversation with Harris and Seldon
Ralph Harris & Arthur Seldon
Occasional Paper 116; ISBN 0 255 36498 9
£7.50

Malaria and the DDT Story
Richard Tren & Roger Bate
Occasional Paper 117; ISBN 0 255 36499 7
£10.00

A Plea to Economists Who Favour Liberty: Assist the Everyman
Daniel B. Klein
Occasional Paper 118; ISBN 0 255 36501 2
£10.00

Waging the War of Ideas
John Blundell
Occasional Paper 119; ISBN 0 255 36500 4
£10.00

The Changing Fortunes of Economic Liberalism

Yesterday, Today and Tomorrow
David Henderson
Occasional Paper 105 (new edition); ISBN 0 255 36520 9
£12.50

The Global Education Industry

Lessons from Private Education in Developing Countries
James Tooley
Hobart Paper 141 (new edition); ISBN 0 255 36503 9
£12.50

Saving Our Streams

The Role of the Anglers' Conservation Association in
Protecting English and Welsh Rivers
Roger Bate
Research Monograph 53; ISBN 0 255 36494 6
£10.00

Better Off Out?

The Benefits or Costs of EU Membership
Brian Hindley & Martin Howe
Occasional Paper 99 (new edition); ISBN 0 255 36502 0
£10.00

Buckingham at 25

Freeing the Universities from State Control
Edited by James Tooley
Readings 55; ISBN 0 255 36512 8
£15.00

Lectures on Regulatory and Competition Policy

Irwin M. Stelzer
Occasional Paper 120; ISBN 0 255 36511 X
£12.50

Misguided Virtue

False Notions of Corporate Social Responsibility
David Henderson
Hobart Paper 142; ISBN 0 255 36510 1
£12.50

HIV and Aids in Schools

The Political Economy of Pressure Groups and Miseducation
Barrie Craven, Pauline Dixon, Gordon Stewart & James Tooley
Occasional Paper 121; ISBN 0 255 36522 5
£10.00

The Road to Serfdom

The Reader's Digest *condensed version*
Friedrich A. Hayek
Occasional Paper 122; ISBN 0 255 36530 6
£7.50

Bastiat's *The Law*

Introduction by Norman Barry
Occasional Paper 123; ISBN 0 255 36509 8
£7.50

A Globalist Manifesto for Public Policy

Charles Calomiris
Occasional Paper 124; ISBN 0 255 36525 X
£7.50

Euthanasia for Death Duties

Putting Inheritance Tax Out of Its Misery
Barry Bracewell-Milnes
Research Monograph 54; ISBN 0 255 36513 6
£10.00

Liberating the Land
The Case for Private Land-use Planning
Mark Pennington
Hobart Paper 143; ISBN 0 255 36508 x
£10.00

IEA Yearbook of Government Performance 2002/ 2003
Edited by Peter Warburton
Yearbook 1; ISBN 0 255 36532 2
£15.00

Britain's Relative Economic Performance, 1870– 1999
Nicholas Crafts
Research Monograph 55; ISBN 0 255 36524 1
£10.00

Should We Have Faith in Central Banks?
Otmar Issing
Occasional Paper 125; ISBN 0 255 36528 4
£7.50

The Dilemma of Democracy
Arthur Seldon
Hobart Paper 136 (reissue); ISBN 0 255 36536 5
£10.00

Capital Controls: a 'Cure' Worse Than the Problem?
Forrest Capie
Research Monograph 56; ISBN 0 255 36506 3
£10.00

The Poverty of 'Development Economics'
Deepak Lal
Hobart Paper 144 (reissue); ISBN 0 255 36519 5
£15.00

Should Britain Join the Euro?
The Chancellor's Five Tests Examined
Patrick Minford
Occasional Paper 126; ISBN 0 255 36527 6
£7.50

Post-Communist Transition: Some Lessons
Leszek Balcerowicz
Occasional Paper 127; ISBN 0 255 36533 0
£7.50

To order copies of currently available IEA papers, or to enquire about availability, please contact:

Lavis Marketing
IEA orders
FREEPOST LON21280
Oxford OX3 7BR

Tel: 01865 767575
Fax: 01865 750079
Email: orders@lavismarketing.co.uk

The IEA also offers a subscription service to its publications. For a single annual payment, currently £40.00 in the UK, you will receive every title the IEA publishes across the course of a year, invitations to events, and discounts on our extensive back catalogue. For more information, please contact:

Subscriptions
The Institute of Economic Affairs
2 Lord North Street
London SW1P 3LB

Tel: 020 7799 8900
Fax: 020 7799 2137
Website: www.iea.org.uk